3/09

WITHDRAWN

GLADIATOR

A TRUE STORY OF 'ROIDS, RAGE,
AND REDEMPTION

DAN CLARK

SCRIBNER

New York   London   Toronto   Sydney

SCRIBNER
A Division of Simon & Schuster, Inc.
1230 Avenue of the Americas
New York, NY 10020

First Scribner hardcover edition February 2009

SCRIBNER and design are registered trademarks of
The Gale Group, Inc., used under license
by Simon & Schuster, Inc., the publisher of this work.

For information about special discounts for bulk purchases,
please contact Simon & Schuster Special Sales:
1-800-456-6798 or business@simonandschuster.com

Designed by Kyoko Watanabe
Text set in Sabon

Manufactured in the United States of America

1   3   5   7   9   10   8   6   4   2

Library of Congress Control Number: 2008048923

ISBN-13: 978-1-4165-9732-2
ISBN-10: 1-4165-9732-8

The names and characteristics of some individuals
have been changed.

All photographs courtesy of the author, except San Jose State 1985
Media Guide cover on p. 46, courtesy of San Jose State University
Athletic Department; and photograph of Mike Adamle, Mike Horton,
Dan Clark, and Larry Csonka, courtesy of Rob Brown.

To my son, my family, and the bright, shining smiles
of my nieces and nephews that became
more important than the roar of the crowd.

Contents

GLADIATOR

Being "Nitro"

Come at me the wrong way tonight and you may not walk out of here alive.

Nitro.

I can't see the audience yet, but I can hear the expectant buzz of excitement as they call out my name. The buildup is infectious. My heart pounds as I pass through the entrance, turn a corner, and catch my first glimpse of thousands and thousands of fans dressed in red, white, and blue. They seem to stretch out forever.

Nitro.

Totally pumped, I burst onto the arena floor of Madison Square Garden as fifteen thousand cheering fans slam to their feet. It is a fantastic world like no other—breathtaking, infinite. I lose myself in the reverberations smashing into each other, a wonderful chaos, as one noise rises above the uncontrolled fervor of screams and whoops. A chant.

NITRO!

All eyes are on me. I luxuriate as the people in the stands lose sight of who they are. Dignity and restraint are tossed aside because standing before them is a hero upon whom they can project their thrills, dreams, and insatiable demands.

NITRO! NITRO! NITRO!

I stand in the midst of the pulsating frenzy, lapping up and sucking in each and every drop.

I look up and catch my breath. There I am, larger-than-life, plastered on the giant JumboTron screen that dangles above the arena like a suspended star.

God, let me die right here.

I begin to run the outer perimeter of the arena in a prebattle ritual. The lyrics to a song by The Who blast from a two-hundred-watt amp and dance in my head.

> *No one knows what it's like*
> *To be the bad man . . .*
> *To be hated*
> *To be fated*
> *To telling only lies*

I spot my opponent for the upcoming event. The hair on the back of my neck and my arms stands up, my heart thumps, and my ears ring loudly with each step toward my opponent—until I am standing across from him.

Like all the ones before him, he is scared. He closes his eyes and sucks in a stiff breath of courage. I can see his eyelids flutter and I sense the terror that churns inside him. He might have been captain of the football team. Hell, he might even have been the best athlete in his state. But now he is standing in front of fifteen thousand people, trying to beat *me*.

He thought he had what it took to get here. He'd put his money where his mouth was, and now he is going to pay the price.

The chant explodes again.

NITRO! NITRO! NITRO!

My body vibrates, my heart rattles against my ribs, and every muscle in my body tightens. I am about to explode into my opponent as hard as I can, to hurt him, to punish him, with my rage and my 235 pounds of solid muscle. At this moment I feel revulsion toward my opponent, absolute hatred. All I want to do is wipe the stupid look off his face.

"Contender, are you ready?" Mike Adamle's voice booms out of the speakers. "Gladiator, are you ready?"

My heart pounds. Louder. Harder. Faster. *Get ready, here I come!*

The whistle blows. I blast into my opponent with reckless abandon, instantly overwhelming and dominating him. My shoulder slams into his ribs, sending the "football captain" flying in the air before landing in a painful, broken heap at my feet. The world slips away, and for a moment the voices are quiet. The universe is mine. Nirvana. The world makes sense. For one moment in time, everything is in sweet, simple order.

This is my refuge, the reason that I compete. It is all about the rush—the hits, the legal acts of physical violence that make the crowd roar and make me grin from ear to ear. The rush lasts for only an infinitesimal period of time, but while it is happening, I revel in a make-believe world where normal rules do not apply. I know that when it is over and the cruel reality of life sets in, the joke will be on me, but I don't care. Everybody craves the incomparable power of being a Gladiator—the potent experience of rising to the heavens, however briefly, igniting and blowing up any dark, hidden places within.

When the referee gives me the victory sign, I fling my arms wide open, tilt back my head, and scream, somehow trying to expose the truth about my beautiful but fucked-up world. The fans are oblivious. I exit the arena while they cheer, and I head into the locker room, where I sit, my head slumped, my body still shooting adrenaline. But even then, when my dreams have become a reality, behind the cheers is a dark secret, a hidden agenda of a life being torn apart and wasted.

I lock myself in an empty stall, and there I am, all alone, the crowd still shrieking from my victory as I sit on the toilet in the shadows and cry for a long time.

Who am I kidding? I know that each time I slam a syringe into my ass or swallow a steroid, it is nobody's fault but my own. I also believe each and every time that I can never stop.

You're asking me why?

Look at the world that has opened up to me.

I have this picture of myself in the back of my head as a chubby kid. And now, girls are hanging on to me, agents wine and dine me, and Warner Bros. wants to make a movie with me.

I pull up to Roxbury, the hottest club in Hollywood. A line of people spills out onto Sunset Boulevard, all waiting to get in. The doorman knows who I am and I slip inside and nod to Sylvester Stallone as I head up the stairs to the VIP room. Everyone is here: Denzel, Van Damme, Snipes, and some rookie seven-foot-two-inch basketball player they call Shaq. The atmosphere is anything-goes. The girls, the armpieces, the hopefuls, the I'll-do-anything-to-get-close-to-celebrity types, pack the room. They're all ripe for the picking. Hell, it is harder to go home alone than it is to take some-one with me.

One afternoon, I'm having lunch at Mezza Luna in Beverly Hills when Steve Martin arrives at my table, introduces himself, and tells me he's a huge fan. As I stand up, shake his hand, and tell him I'm *his* biggest fan, he brings me over to Dustin Hoffman's table and introduces me to the actor and his wife. A few nights later, I'm at the home of the late billionaire Marvin Davis. Tony Bennett is the enter-tainment, and Cristal Champagne is on ice as I'm introduced to for-mer presidents Ford and Carter. As I'm leaving, Merv Griffin calls out, "Dan, there's someone I want you to meet." It's Ronald Reagan.

———

I was living the all-expenses-paid life everyone dreams about. I could walk into any place in Hollywood like I was a fucking movie star. I went from looking at the world to watching the world look at me.

The thing is, I love my country. I'm proud to have been the star of a show with the word *American* in the title. *American Gladiators*. A hit show that aired in more than forty countries with over 12 million weekly viewers. Madison Square Garden was the first stop in our 150-city live tour and I loved it, but somewhere inside, I knew it was all a lie, that I was deceiving people. But I told myself it was okay because they didn't really want the truth. They wanted to be entertained. That I was addicted to steroids, drugs that not only altered my consciousness but also altered my appearance, was the secret hook that drew the crowds, and everybody ate it up. If only someone had told me the truth back then when I was Nitro and thought I was indestructible.

Of course, the question is, would I have listened? Would I have done things differently if I'd known then what I know today? It's hard to say, but these days you should see me wake up in the morning . . . or maybe you shouldn't. As a result of twenty years of steroid use, I walk with a limp, I have seven scars on my face, two destroyed knees, and I can't walk up a flight of stairs until I chug a couple of cups of black coffee and a handful of anti-inflammatory pills. What strapping eighteen-year-old athlete could ever imagine ending up with a herniated back disk and a neck that pops like fireworks on the Fourth of July from a mere turn of my head? And those are the obvious problems. The *real* prizes are a pair of shrunken testicles and surgical scars across my nipples from having breast tissue removed from my chest.

It wasn't always like this . . .

CHAPTER 1

In Search of an Identity

What are the worst three words a child can hear?

We're getting divorced.

I am four years old in 1968, and my father has just returned to California from a two-year work stint in Vietnam. He walks into the living room of our box-size home in the severely depressed belly of Orange County, California, and announces, "Your mother and I are getting a divorce. You and your brother are going to Minnesota with me. Your sister is staying here with your mom." My father, Wally, is massive, forceful, and relentless. We are all insignificant and powerless in his wake.

So this is it. No explaining. No comforting. No choices. My brother, Randy, two years older than me, is my idol. My hero. My rock. My chubby-cheeked, ebullient little sister, Christine, is two years my junior.

My mother, Kazuko, whom my father met while he was in the marines in Japan, can do little to protest. She's been in the United States for only a short time, barely speaks English, and doesn't understand the customs and laws of this country. She doesn't know it's customary for the mother to get custody of the kids, and she doesn't know my father's threats of deportation are empty slings of intimidation.

A few days later, I'm standing in the airplane aisle watching the flight attendant closing the plane doors. I'm squeezing my eyes shut as hard as I can, with nothing but the blindness of hope that I can still keep this divorce nightmare from happening. That is when I still dreamed. That is when I thought I could make a difference. That is when I still believed. A flight attendant approaches me, shattering the illusion: "Young man, you're going to have to sit down."

I open my eyes to discover I'm still on the plane with my father and my brother already seated to my side. I see my mother, her eyes full of sorrow, on the tarmac holding my two-year-old sister.

"Sit down," my father barks.

I shake my head no. I am making a stand. Somehow at that young age, I instinctively know if I sit, life as I know it will be over. I glance over at my brother and think, why isn't he protesting? He's older and he should just tell everyone we're not doing it. This doesn't work for us. We're not leaving my mother and sister.

My dad glares at me, the threat of violence in his voice. "Sit down!"

I stand my ground, even though I am *deathly* afraid of him. I know I'm somewhat safe because he won't hit me in public. Now everyone is staring at me. I'm sobbing as I watch my mom and my sister disappear from the tarmac. *No, don't leave. Don't go! I need you. Stay! Fight! Fight for me!* The door is shut and I start sobbing even harder.

A man in an aisle seat across from my father leans over and says: "Big boys don't cry."

Are you kidding me? Big boys don't cry? I'm four years old, my family has just been torn apart. I don't know when I'll see my mother or sister again. And this ridiculous, idiotic statement is supposed to make me stop crying?

Well, it works.

That, and he asks me to flex my muscle. I squeeze my arm tight and up springs this little bud of a biceps. The man acts impressed and makes gushing sounds of admiration. "Wow, you see that?" he asks. I nod that I do and he says, "You're a big boy, and big boys don't cry." I get the message loud and clear at the tender age of four: Muscles make you strong and invulnerable. When you're a boy, the quickest way to become a man is not to cry.

My brother and I spend almost five years in Minnesota, from 1968 to 1972, but not with my father. He dropped us off on his way back to Vietnam and we lived with my father's brother, Uncle Ron, and his wife, Barbara. The most important thing you need to know about Minnesota is that we were wanted. Ron and Barbara couldn't have children, so they treat us as if we are their own. They do everything they can to make us feel like we are not just a couple of kids dumped on their doorstep.

We do family things. In the winter we play hockey and sled; in the spring, baseball; the fall, football. We take family drives in the convertible, my brother and me squished in the back between two giant collies, the wind blowing in our hair, the world rushing by us. We are free and happy.

In the fall of my second year in Minnesota, my mom and her new husband, John, drive 1,933 miles cross-country, from California to Minnesota, in a Ford Pinto with a defective, exploding gas tank, to visit us. She couldn't afford to fly so she saved up for two years and has to sleep in the car on the way, but she makes it.

You see, the Japanese culture frowns on being overly expressive, emotional, or affectionate, so Mom prefers to bow rather than get tangled up in an embrace. To this day, when I try to wrap her up in a big hug, she stiffens up like a board.

In Minnesota, every time my older brother leaves the house, my aunt hollers, "Take your little brother with you!" Randy races off on his bike a little faster than he knows I can pedal, and I struggle mightily to keep up with him. But he never goes fast enough to lose me. It's just a typical big-brother-torturing-his-little-brother thing and *I know he loves me*. He can do or say whatever he wants to me, but if anyone else lays a finger on me or says anything inappropriate, he'll have the kid clenched in a headlock in no time, making him apologize to his little brother. Every touchdown my brother scores, every home run he hits, I stand off to the side and watch, knee-deep in envy and admiration, hoping and praying that one day I'll grow up to be just like him.

Time flies by in Minnesota. In 1972, we've been there for four years and we're happy. We've finally accepted this as our home when the unthinkable happens on a crisp Saturday morning. Randy and I are playing "kill the guy with the football" in our front yard with a couple of kids from the neighborhood when a taxi pulls up. A man exits and walks toward us.

Our father.

When he sees us, he drops to one knee, opens his arms wide, and bellows, "Hey, boys! It's your dad." Neither of us moves. He is our father but he is a stranger to us. For the last four years, we have received not one phone call or letter from him.

He calls out again, "Hey, boys! Come say hello to your father!" I look at Randy for a cue on how to proceed. I see the contempt in his eyes, he isn't moving. The next thing I know, I'm walking toward my father and hugging him. I don't know if I feel sorry for him or if I actually want to hug him.

Later that night in our bedroom, Randy gives me an earful. "Look, he can't just come back here and think he's going to be our dad and that everything is all right."

"But at least he came back," I say.

"It just doesn't work that way," Randy says, frustrated with me. "You're too young, you just don't get it." The admonition hurts, but he's right. I didn't get it. Maybe that's the difference in the mind-set of an eight-year-old and a ten-year-old, or maybe it's simply the difference in our personalities. He's the leader and I'm the follower.

As we sit huddled in our bedroom, we can hear Ron and Barbara arguing with our dad. Things went well for him in Vietnam. He quit his job at the engineering plant, he opened a successful American restaurant in Saigon that served homesick GIs, and he wanted to take us to Vietnam with him. Ron and Barb rise up in fierce opposition. They don't think it's safe for us there and they desperately want us to stay with them. My dad refuses to listen in spite of the horrific headlines plastered across the papers of bombings, bloodshed, and dead soldiers.

"We're Americans," my dad says proudly. "We've never lost a war and we're not going to lose this one."

A few days later, my brother and I are on a plane to Vietnam—one more journey in a long line of trips about which I had no choice. I don't cry when the doors close this time, but I am scared to death. The night before we left, a kid named Michael Johnson from the neighborhood told me his oldest brother went to Vietnam and never came back. They sent his mom a flag, instead.

Randy tells me, "Michael Johnson's brother was a soldier in the war. They don't kill kids there." He promises he won't let anything happen to me. We promise each other we'll always stick together, no matter what.

The airplane lands, the door swings open. I exit the craft and stand at the top of the steps, sweating from the blistering heat. I squint, trying to see through the bright summer sun to get a glimpse of my new home. Silhouetted figures skitter below us. I blink again, and slowly the world comes into view as I see soldiers strapped with M16 rifles littering the tarmac. We step off the plane, walk into the terminal, and I stop in front of a soldier. I've never seen a real gun up close. It is frightening and exhilarating to be inches from a hunk of hardened metal that could play God.

As we drive away from the airport, the sounds and the sights of this new, bizarre world rush in. The streets are filled with the chaos of cyclo mais, taxis, bicycles, and cars. Pedestrians pack the sidewalks, and everyone is in a mad but civilized rush. We arrive at our new house, where a host of people are waiting for us. My dad leads us to a petite Asian woman in her thirties.

"Boys, this is your new mom, Kimm," Dad says.

Kimm cracks a down-turned smile. It's immediately clear that having us come here wasn't her idea. From behind this hardened woman steps a cute five-year-old girl with a white ribbon in her hair. "This is your sister Debbie," Dad says.

I'm stunned to find out I have a sister here, and her radiant smile immediately wins me over. Living in Vietnam in 1972 is like living in New York in the weeks following 9/11. You can smell the fear, the uneasiness, the despair, which to an eight-year-old boy is both glorious and hellish.

After about a year, the U.S. government pulls the majority of its troops out of Vietnam, and my father loses the majority of his clientele. To keep his business afloat, he puts a couple of blackjack tables upstairs above the restaurant and brings "tea girls" (prostitutes) to the bar. When a customer sits down at the bar, the girls try to strike up a conversation and to get him to buy them a $15 glass of tea. The girls get a cut from the drinks, so the more overpriced drinks the customers buy, the more money the girls make.

I recognize the art form in it. The girls who do best make the men feel as if they genuinely like and are interested in them. You do this for a man, he'll open up his wallet for you. If a customer wants to do more than drink, he talks to the old mama-san who looks after the girls and makes an arrangement to take her home for the night for about $30.

I don't end up losing my virginity to a tea girl, even though they constantly heckle me, calling me "cherry boy" and telling me how they want to "pop my cherry." At ten years old, I desperately want that, too, but I don't have any hair down there and there's no way in hell I'm going to let a girl see what my dad commonly refers to as "peach fuzz."

My dad is a womanizer. If he could keep his dick in his pants, he could save himself a lot of trouble and money, but he doesn't feel that he has to live by the same rules as everyone else. He simply follows his desires and is a victim of his appetites. It was no surprise, then, that in November 1974 his gallivanting ways got him into trouble. Dad is seeing a young waitress named Tu who works at the restaurant. Kimm finds out and kicks Randy and me out of the house, putting us in a cab that takes us to Charlie Brown's, another American restaurant in Saigon.

We wait there, and hours later my dad shows up and takes us to his friend's house, just outside the city. "You'll be staying here at the colonel's house for a while," he tells us. But a week later, he informs us he's sending us back to the States. He doesn't give us a reason, and I don't think, at ten, I'd have understood if he had. But looking back, I believe it was because the situation in Vietnam had deteriorated so badly it was no longer safe for us to remain there. I also believe somewhere in his heart my dad knew that he wasn't doing a great job as a father, and it would be best to send us to someone who could raise us better—another stunning change over which I have no say. But as long as I'm going with Randy, that is enough for me.

The day before we're scheduled to leave, I became what I am today.

Randy and I are alone on the rooftop patio of the colonel's three-story cement block of a home. My father and his new girlfriend, Tu, have gone into the city to buy supplies for our trip home. Randy doesn't want to leave because he has fallen hard for a teenage girl he met a few weeks earlier. He is heartbroken over never seeing her again. I'm drawing a picture of an airplane as a sudden gust of wind whooshes by, lifting my picture in the air.

It lands on a thick rope of electrical cable on the other side of the four-foot wall that encompasses the perimeter of the roof. "I'll get it," Randy says as he hops over the wall, landing on a two-foot ledge. He's three stories up with nothing in front of him but air. The picture is draped across the eye-level-high wire, fluttering in the wind.

Filled with the spirit of Bruce Lee, Randy grabs the wall behind him for support and kicks out, trying to hit the paper. He misses. "Damn! I can't reach it," he groans.

"Bruce Lee could reach it," I say, egging him on.

Randy kicks out with all of his strength and connects with the paper—and the wire.

Then it happens. A flash of electrical discharge and a loud popping noise as a sudden jolt of electricity surges through Randy's body with such force it knocks him back against the wall. He starts to fall forward, and instinctively to prevent himself from falling three stories, he reaches out and grabs the wire with both hands.

A shower of sparks. The crackling of electricity. Randy's body shakes and convulses as seventy-five thousand volts of electricity course through him.

"Let go!" I scream. *"LET GO!"*

The electricity continues to rattle his body as the sparks fizzle, and a thick, white smoke fills the air with the stench of burnt flesh.

Please let go!

Randy is suddenly buffeted back, slammed against the wall, and he disappears from view.

"Randy! Randy!" I scream and race forward, praying that he didn't fall all the way to the ground. I peer over the wall and see my brother slumped over on his side, unconscious, having barely managed to stay on the ledge. Then I notice his fingers, burnt to stubs. Fragments of white bone are visible through charcoal-black flesh that extends all the way up to his wrists. The bottom of the tennis shoe on the foot he kicked the wire with has melted, and burnt flesh protrudes through the opening.

I lean over the wall, reach down, and grab Randy with both hands, trying to lift him back over the wall. I'm not strong enough. I try again, but I can't do it. "C'mon, Randy, you gotta help me!"

I plead as I try again. And again, I'm not strong enough. I scream in frustration and hold my brother tight against the wall. Scared . . . not knowing what to do . . . not wanting to let go of him . . . hugging him . . . loving him . . . needing him.

I spot three men working in the street below. I yell at them, but they're too far away to hear me. I gently release my brother, making sure he stays on the ledge, then I race downstairs to the street where the men are working.

"You've got to help me! It's my brother! I help me please!" No one moves. They just look at me. I scream at them again. "You have to help me! Please . . . *chet*" ("dead" in Vietnamese). "My brother, *chet*." Still nothing. They don't speak English. I grab one of the men by the shirt and start dragging him violently toward the house, saying, "Come! Come now!" in Vietnamese.

Two of the men finally get it and start to follow me. We charge into the house and race up the stairs to the roof. I jerk the men toward the wall. With their help, we lift my brother over and lay his rigid body on the tile floor. My eyes flick across the workers as they check Randy's vitals. I'll never forget the sickening hum like a mad swarm of bees that fills the air and exists under everything. I don't know where it's coming from.

"*Chet . . . Chet?*" I ask.

The men don't know and continue frantically to check my brother's body. I feel the tears welling up in my eyes. I'm going to cry.

But, no . . . *Big boys don't cry.*

I fight back my tears. A single droplet threatens to escape over the brim of my eyelid and spill down my cheek. I blink furiously, sucking in large breaths between gritted teeth, feeling somehow that my brother's fate hangs in the balance of my keeping that tear from falling.

Don't cry! Don't cry!

Don't die! Don't die!

One of the men suddenly looks at me and in broken English says, "Ho-sp-tal." My heart jumps. That meant he's alive and there's something worth saving. The men indicate they need my help to carry my brother down the stairs. I rise and stand over my brother, looking down at him. His face is undamaged and still beautiful, but his body is rigid . . . not flaccid as it should be. I know there is a word for this . . . *rigor* . . . *rigor* . . . something . . . but isn't that only after someone has been dead for a while?

The sickening buzzing sound continues to permeate the air. I can't figure out where it's coming from as I try to quiet my mind— millions of thoughts crashing into each other. I kneel down and slide my hands underneath by brother's shoulder to help lift him. My face is inches from his. Then I realize that the haunting hum is coming out of his open mouth. It's the sound of seventy-five thousand volts of electricity coursing through his charred body.

At the hospital, I stand outside the primitively equipped operating room and watch through a window as a team of doctors works frantically on Randy. He is still in his clothes and has a host of tubes coming out of him. My dad and Tu are there as well. Dad, disjointed and in bad shape, mumbles something about taking Randy to the Mayo Clinic . . . and how it'd be the best place to get skin grafts for his hands and feet.

"Dad, is he going to be okay?" I ask.

"I'm not sure . . . but . . . I think so," he answers as he wipes back his tears.

I nod, push away from the window, and walk down the hall. I am angry. Furious. Full of more rage than my little ten-year-old body can handle. *You idiot. This is your fault! If you hadn't let that stupid paper blow away, Randy would be okay.* I pray to God and thank him for keeping my brother alive. That's when out of the corner of my eye—

I see my dad move closer to the window, a look of horror on his face. Something is terribly wrong. I run back to the emergency room and look through the window to see a doctor with both hands on Randy's chest, frantically trying to get his heart to beat again. Blood has formed at the side of his mouth and his face is turning blue. The EKG flatlines. A doctor jumps on him and starts to pound on his chest, desperately trying to revive him.

Still the *flatline*.

Two doctors finally stop him from pumping on my brother's chest. He climbs off Randy and looks at us for a long, chill moment. My dad begins to weep. *But you were talking about . . . going to the Mayo Clinic? I thought he was . . . he was . . . going to be okay.* Then reality slowly begins sinking in.

But he can't be . . . he can't be . . .

My father crumples to his knees, buries his face in his hands, and sobs uncontrollably. I don't cry. I can't cry. I run as fast as my little legs will carry me and find refuge around the corner, where I pummel a wall with both fists in blind rage.

Please, God! Let Randy live.

He's stronger . . . smarter. Better than me.

He deserves to live, not me.

Please take me instead, God.

Please, God . . . take me.

It's the last time I pray.

My father doesn't want to bury Randy in Vietnam. He wants to send him back to the United States, but there is too much political red tape. It will take over a month to get his body back home. My dad decides to bury Randy in Saigon, in a cemetery that is exclusively for wealthy Vietnamese and French dignitaries. This all happens during the peace treaty. I don't think anyone thought we'd lose the war and have to evacuate the country.

The funeral is held in a Buddhist shrine. I stand over Randy's open casket gazing down at his pale, inert face. I can't get over how peaceful he looks. How *beautiful* he looks. It is nearly impossible to believe that Randy, my beautiful twelve-year-old brother, is *dead*.

The Buddhist monks chatter in excitement over a moth that has landed on Randy's casket. They believe it is my brother incarnate.

I stare at them as a myriad of emotions runs through me, but no tears.

I keep thinking, *Big boys don't cry. Big boys don't cry.*

Then another thought pops into my head: *Big boys don't die. Big boys don't die.*

Randy was big. Bigger than I could ever be. If he died, then what in the world was going to happen to me?

When I am ten years old . . .

I see my dad bloody and beat the shit out of a guy.

I see my dad writhing on the floor, suffering a heart attack.

I see my dad beat the shit out of my brother.

I see my dad cry and drink himself to oblivion after my brother's death.

I see my dad fuck two prostitutes while I lie in the same bed.

I see my father wave good-bye to me as I board the plane to return to the United States, alone.

I became what I am in a shower of sparks when I was ten years old.
At my brother's funeral with my dad and little sister Debbie.

CHAPTER 2

Living in La-La Land

In November 1974, I return from Vietnam to live in California with my mother, my sister, and my mom's husband, John. There's also a new addition to the family, a little brother named John-John. Still grieving over Randy's death, I'm disconnected and isolated. I feel a perpetual sense of loss. The world is spinning around me at dizzying speeds, while I feel stuck in time.

My stepdad, John, takes me to the local park for baseball try-outs. He thinks sports will be a good way for me to make friends. All the ten-year-olds start off in the outfield, shagging fly balls. My turn comes. I lift my glove up to catch the fly ball. It flutters in the wind. I move left . . . then right. Crack! It hits me in the forehead. I grab my face and run off the field buried in humiliation.

Some gladiator I am—some heroic gladiator.

John isn't embarrassed in the slightest. He puts his arm around me, leads me to the car, and says, "Don't worry about it. We'll get 'em next time." John is a good man who treats me like his own son and goes out of his way to make me feel comfortable and a part of something. My mom is the same way. But a lot of times I catch her staring at me with tears in her eyes. I'm not sure if she's glad that I'm alive or she's sad because my brother is dead. We never talk about it. That kind of emotional expression isn't part of her Japanese culture, but I never fail to see the fear and pain in her eyes. I don't understand what it means until I'm a grown man, glance in the mirror, and see the same look staring back at me.

My father never discusses my brother's death with me, either. We didn't have one of those "It's going to be hard on you, Son, but just hang in there and things will get better—" or "I love you, Son, don't worry, we're going to get through this. I'm going to keep you safe" or even "I'm sorry."

Living in the shadows, cut off from the world, I find my identity playing sports. Football. The elementary savagery appeals to me—something to do with the violence and being able to hit someone without getting in trouble. I'm not talking about punching someone with your fists. I'm talking about throwing every ounce of your being at another person with reckless abandon, then going back to the huddle and then doing it all over again. I also like the idea of anonymity, being hidden under a helmet and shoulder pads. I'm not confident of my ability and I don't like being in the spotlight. I feel, for better or worse, that the football field is a place I can hide out in relative obscurity.

I'm wrong.

I can't make the weight restrictions for ten-year-olds and am quickly thrust into the spotlight as the "chubby kid" who's too fat to play. I want to quit, but my mom and John won't let me because money is tight and they've already paid the season fee for me and for my little sister, Christine, to be a cheerleader.

I practice with the team all week, dreading the rapidly approaching weekend when we have the weigh-in before each game. Each week I get on the scale in my underwear, my little gut protruding, and each week I watch as the scale tips over the weight limit. It's embarrassing. I go from getting hit in the face with the baseball to being too fat to play football.

Finally, I've had enough. I go on a diet. Three weeks later I make the weight. I can play in my first game, or at least that's what I think. That week, we play the first-place team. I stand on the sidelines, helmet on, ready to go, making sure to stay close to the coach, so he can find me. The entire game I shadow him.

"Clark, get outta my way!" he hollers as he trips over me.

"Yes, sir!" I shout back as I continue to stalk him.

Wherever he turns, I'm there. Ready. Waiting. It's the fourth quarter, a close game, and I still haven't played. I look at my mom and John on the sidelines sitting in their chairs watching. I look at the clock, hope spilling out of me by the second. But he has to play me, right? That's the rule. It states that all eligible boys have to play in the game. The other team scores and goes ahead. We drive down the field, getting ready to score and take the lead with thirty seconds left. I realize I'm not going to get in when my stepdad stands and yells, "Hey, my kid hasn't been in!"

"Next week!" the coach screams back.

Then the next thing I know, John, all six feet three inches, 235 pounds of him, is up out of his seat, charging toward the coach, yelling, "Look, every kid gets to play. It's a rule!" The coach starts to respond, but John gets in his face. "Don't say anything! I want him in there now! He deserves to play!" I'm stunned and deeply moved. I can't believe John's standing up for me.

Thirty years later, I would stare down at John in his hospital bed and gaze into his tired eyes, drawn narrow from drinking, and thank him for that moment. He doesn't say anything; the cancer eating away his liver is too much for him. Jaundiced and weak, he squeezes my hand and smiles sadly, then closes his eyes. He dies a few days later. I don't think he ever knows how monumental that moment was for me. It was the building block, the first step that helped me cross the ocean of life. It taught me that I was of value and worth fighting for.

———

The next few years are rocky. Dad has been back in the States for a couple of years. He has a house in Santa Ana, California, and he wants me to come live with him. He bribes me with an offer of my own room with a stereo in it. Both are luxuries to a kid now sharing a tiny room with his younger brother. More important, this is the first time I actually get to make a choice. It's up to me where I'm going to live. After my freshman year, I decide to go live with my father. There have been two additions to the family. A sister named Michelle, and a brother, Kevin.

In my sophomore year I finally become a starter on the football field. That same year, I win my first MVP award at Saddleback High School. I'm the absolute best football player in the tenth grade. I've finally found something I'm good at. I've finally found a way to shine. I've finally found my identity. I'm a football player.

Football is more than a game to me. I love the attention, the adulation. It's like an opiate—and my pursuit of it becomes a ruthless obsession. When you're a high school football star, you're the king of the campus. Everyone envies you. You're invited to the hottest parties, and you get the best girls. Being a football player opens doors that other students only dream of.

I consistently push myself beyond what I think is possible. All

I think and dream about is playing football. I spend more time at the practice field than I do at home. Some days I don't know if I'm going to make it anymore, days in the sweltering summer sun running sprints until I puke, days in the sweaty weight room pounding out rep after rep, until I can't move. But the image of standing in front of the crowd bathed in adoration keeps me going.

My senior year, I win my second MVP award and feel like the world belongs to me. I discover how successful I can be when I free myself from the constant self doubt that has been with me since the death of my brother. But then reality thunders in like a slap in the face. I don't receive a single scholarship offer. Sure, recruiters come by . . . but there's always an excuse, too short, too slow, too small, too few scholarships. It brings back a lot of memories of being the fat kid who is always picked last.

I sit in the empty bleachers of the football stadium in the waning summer sun, wondering if the dream is over. Is high school really going to be the best years of my life, the time against which all other moments will be compared? I hate the thought. Empty places loom large inside me that nothing can fill but the sounds of the entire student body cheering wildly for me on the football field.

I remember at the beginning of my senior year, how much time I thought I had. And then, just like that, it's over—finished. I'm no longer a high school football player, but a seventeen-year-old kid who has absolutely no idea what I'm going to do with my life. But this somehow fits into the way I see the world. At a young age, I've already learned to be wary of making plans. They can't be trusted.

Six months after the football season ends, I'm still lost and contemplating my future. I can always try to walk on at a school, but my grades are only decent, and my family can't afford tuition anywhere. I get depressed and upset for allowing myself to think I could have gotten a scholarship. Yet in my heart, I know I'm not done yet. I still have a lot of fight in me.

There *has* to be a place for me.

"Junior college," my coach says as I sit across from him in the football office. "Santa Ana JC is only a couple of miles away, and they've got a really good football program."

Junior college isn't part of the plan. I always thought junior college was a vocational school, or a place for continuing adult education, not a place to play football. Coach makes me promise that I'll at least swing by the campus to check it out.

I go and see the football coach the following week. As I strut across campus, junior college looks like high school with ashtrays. But it's college and they have a football team, and players are getting rides to Division I schools. I think, if that's what it's going to take to keep this dream alive, then I'm going to do it.

I pound the weights all summer. By the time the season starts, I'm six feet two inches, 210 pounds of lean, ripped muscle, and running a 4.6 in the forty-yard dash. I definitely have the requisite size and speed to play big-time college football. Now all I have to do is show the scouts I can play. What I don't know is that Santa Ana is one of the top junior colleges in the nation for football. It's littered with athletes just like me, and *better* than me, from all over the country, who, for one reason or another, didn't get a scholarship. It's a rogues' gallery of misfits.

I start off the season on the bench, but it doesn't bother me. In fact I like being the underdog. I like the odds stacked up against me. I don't know it any other way. But I know I'll prevail simply because I want it more than anyone else.

As the season progresses, with each game the prospect of getting a scholarship gets better and better. It's real. Tangible. A couple of sophomores have already signed letters of intent to big Division I schools, and I'm now in the starting lineup, playing just as well as they are, if not better. We have two games left. Scouts from all over the country are supposed to be here tonight. This could be my final home game at Santa Ana if I go out there and have a hell of a game.

I stand under the bright stadium lights, burning with intensity, ready to pour out my heart and soul on the field. The rest of the team spills out of the locker room, and we congregate behind a huge banner made by the cheerleaders, yelling, screaming, and pounding on each other's pads. With a deafening roar, we charge through the banner and I burst onto the field of dreams, running toward a brilliant future that awaits me.

On the first play of the game, I explode off the line, blitz unimpeded toward the quarterback, when the running back dives for my knees. Crack! The pain shoots in, overwhelming my senses. There's a moment of disorientation everything seems to slow I exist only in my head and I can't believe it's actually happening to me as I collapse to the ground. My eyes blink open but darkness still rules. The world starts to come back fast and furious. Bodies, thick and padded, are crashing into and piling on top of me. All I can think is *My knee, my fucking knee!* I scream, *"Get off of me!"* but nobody moves. I'm helpless, lost under the mountain of bodies, suffering . . . waiting. A whistle blows. People start to climb to their feet, yet I remain on the ground, my promising football career assassinated by a vicious blow to the knee.

A million thoughts go through my mind: *Am I going to be all right? Will I be able to play again? How bad is it? It's over. Fuck, it's over!*

I feel my dreams slipping away from me, years of hard work gone in the blink of an eye. The trainer and the coach hover over me, backlit by the stadium lights. I don't know if they're angels or devils. All I want is to hear the magic words, *You're going to be okay.* They help me to my feet, I try to walk, but I can't. A couple of my teammates come over and carry me off the field.

The pain in my knee is just a dull thud, but my head throbs, continually bombarded with thoughts: *My career is over. It's fucking over! Oh, my God, what am I going to do?* A part of me is buoyed by the possibility that the doctor will give me good news, but inside I know the truth. My gut never lies. *This is bad.* I bury that thought, and the first words to the doctor are always the same: "I'm going to be all right, aren't I?"

That night I'm lying in a hospital bed, waiting for God to speak to me. I'm not talking about the Father, Son, Holy Ghost kind of God. I'm talking about the guy in the white jacket who's examining my knee. Right now, he's God and he holds my future in his hands.

The prognosis isn't as bad as I expect. I have torn cartilage in my knee. What a relief. The doctor explains the arthroscopic-surgery procedure. Basically, they make a couple of small incisions in the knee, insert a camera, and do all the repairing from there without ever having to open up the knee. The benefit is the healing time. He assures me this one should be a snap. The last words I remember him saying to me before I go under are "You might be able to play in the last game of the season." I smile, counting backward, ninety-nine, ninety-eight, ninety-seven . . . ninety-six . . . and I'm out.

I wake up in the hospital room alone, disoriented and sick to my stomach from the anesthesia. I have no idea how many hours have passed. I try to move my injured leg. It feels oddly heavy. I know something is wrong. I rip back the covers and stare, horrified, at my leg. It's in a cast from my thigh all the way down to my foot. Thoughts run through my head. *What the hell happened? Am I going to be okay? Where the hell is the doctor?*

My hand reaches out for help and falls short of the button to call the nurse as my panic continues to grow. Finally I scream, "Help me!"

A nurse comes rushing in. "What's the matter?"

"Where's the doctor?" I yell. "Get me the doctor!"

"He's gone for the night and won't be back until the morning," she says.

"What do you mean he's gone?"

She looks at me blankly. I have a million questions and I start asking them. Why do I have a cast on? What did he do to me? Am I going to be able to play again?

She doesn't answer any of my questions. She tells me she isn't allowed to say anything. It's up to the doctor to tell me what's happening. I'm furious, about to rip her head off. *Fuck the rules and tell me what happened! It's my knee! It's my career! It's my future! It's my life!*

My girlfriend comes rushing in. In a fugue of postoperative anesthesia, I bury my face into her and sob quietly. My sister comes in shortly after and comforts me as well. To this day, twenty-five years later, that was the only time my sister ever saw me cry. Shamefully, it was about my knee. It wasn't about my brother dying or my dad dying. It was about . . . my knee.

The next day, the doctor tells me there were complications, so he was forced to cut my knee open to remove all of the lateral meniscus cartilage, as well as shave off a portion of the medial meniscus. I won't be playing football for a while or even be able to start rehabbing the knee for six weeks. It sounds like a death sentence to me. He might as well have told me I had a terminal illness.

I watch the last game of the season from the sidelines, hobbling on crutches, aching because I want and need to be playing. I feel a coldness snake through me. My dream is dying, and all I can do is watch, lost in the roars of the crowd; cheers that had once been for me. The hard-earned muscle I've gained over the years falls off my body in the next six weeks. I get down to 178 pounds, hardly a college prospect. This sends me into a horrible depression. I started off as a nobody, and through hard work and determination I found an identity as an athlete. Now I'm losing it. My injury isn't only derailing my football career, it's stealing my definition of who I am. I've swiftly gone from feeling like a somebody to a nobody—a complete loser.

This makes me more determined than ever to rebuild my muscle and be a star the very next year. As soon as I get the okay, I begin to rehab like a madman. The process is excruciatingly slow and grueling. It takes me two to three months just to put a few pounds back on, and I know that at this rate I'll never be ready for football season—until I meet Joe.

CHAPTER 3

Gym Candy

I'm working out in the gym in 1982 when I meet a guy, Joe, twenty years old, huge, ripped, and looking absolutely awesome. He is my Faust, my Iago. Everyone in the gym stares at and admires his physique. Over the next few weeks I get to know Joe a little bit, and when I feel comfortable, I ask him his secret to getting huge.

His eyes light up; he leans forward and whispers a magic word in my ear. A secret that would change everything.

"Steroids."

I have no idea what he's talking about. I've never even heard the word before. "What the hell are steroids?" I ask.

He smirks, sure that I'm being disingenuous. "Come on, you know what I'm talking about. The juice, the bean, gear, sauce, gym candy."

I still don't have any idea what he's referring to. You have to remember it's 1982 and Arnold Schwarzenegger and Lou Ferrigno (the Incredible Hulk) have just exploded onto the national body-building scene. This is way before the public's awareness of steroids, when everyone thought these massively built men were freaks of nature who engaged in insane training rituals that turned them into heroic, unbeatable icons of strength and stamina.

Joe tells me that steroids are hormones that help the body rebuild, so you can train harder and recover sooner. He assures me taking steroids *isn't cheating,* far from it. Steroids simply give you the ability to work harder. But I'm a pessimist when it comes to things that seem too good to be true.

"What's the catch?" I ask.

"There are none," he says. "It's a new experimental thing that a few bright doctors are testing. They can help your knee injury heal and help you pack on the pounds for the upcoming season."

"C'mon. There's gotta be a catch," I say.

He laughs. "Okay, there *is* one catch. You're going to get freaky strong, real fast, on them."

Part of me wants to punch him in the face, thinking he's toying with me. But he goes on to tell me that a lot of pro football players are on them, and that steroids are legal and safe. They have to be. He got them from a doctor.

I know right away that steroids are for me. I can't wait to get them, or anything else that'll get me ready for the season. I don't feel like it's necessary to ask anyone's permission, but I still tell my dad about the drugs that night. He's okay with it, especially since it's under a doctor's supervision.

I make my appointment to see the steroid doctor on the next Saturday. Since his office is up in San Gabriel Valley, an hour away, Joe volunteers to drive. On Friday night I'm so excited I can hardly sleep as I fantasize how steroids will make everything in my life perfect again. I'll start to perform on the field, I'll get the attention, and I'll be somebody.

Joe arrives bright and early on Saturday as promised. I meet him at the door, hat in hand, ready to go. As we leave the house, he tells me to make sure to bring my driver's license to show the doctor I'm eighteen. I stop in my tracks. Joe assumes I'm eighteen because I'm in college, but I'll actually be seventeen for six more weeks. Joe and I rush into the house to get my dad to write a note saying I have parental consent. My dad is totally down with writing something for me, if that's what I want. Hell, he thinks, anything for me to be the best I can be.

I clutch the note, and as we roll up the freeway to San Gabriel Valley, I keep urging Joe to step on it. When we arrive, I rush into the doctor's office. The receptionist politely asked for my ID. I confidently flipped it out with the note from my father, but she takes one look at it and shoots me down. It isn't going to happen. I have to be eighteen. I return home crushed.

During the next few weeks, I watch with envy as Joe trains and grows even bigger and harder. My mind is made up; I have to get steroids. I try to convince Joe to give me some of his, but he won't. He believes they have to be done under a doctor's supervision. And now there's a new caveat. He says that Dr. Kerr won't prescribe steroids to just anyone. He only provides them to people with "special needs." I'm not sure what that means. What "special need" does Joe have? But I'm not concerned. I know that once I tell Dr. Kerr my situation, he'll give me the goods. My injury has to be enough.

The day I turn eighteen, I walk back into Dr. Kerr's office. My birthday present from my dad is the $125 for my first visit, which should cover the steroids the doctor will hopefully prescribe. The receptionist leads me to a back room and tells me the doctor will be in shortly. I sit on the table, taking in the room, surprised by how small and plain it is. When the doctor walks in, I feel like Dorothy in the *Wizard of Oz*. I'm finally getting to see the great wizard, and he turns out to be an ordinary-looking man. *Please let him have the magic,* I think.

Dr. Kerr goes through the orientation with me: "Steroids are synthetic derivatives of testosterone—the hormone that makes a man a man. They help you build muscle by increasing the anabolic process of the body, as well as the androgenic qualities, which refers to the secondary sex characteristics. You'll put on size, strength, and mass, and you'll be an animal on the football field."

It sounds so good. "Why isn't everyone using them?" I ask.

He smiles and says, "They will be." He tells me that I'll be taking an injectable steroid called testosterone cypionate and an oral steroid called Dianabol.

"What are the risks?"

"The orals are more effective, but harder on the body because they put a lot of strain on the liver, where they get processed. To counter that, we take an injectable that has more of the androgenic properties. There *can* be some testicular atrophy, but in the small doses you're taking, I don't think it'll be a problem. Also, there are rare cases of gynecomastia."

"Gyno what?"

"Gynecomastia. Your body may produce estrogen to balance the high testosterone. It's rare, and everyone has a different tolerance to the particular steroids."

I look at him confused. I don't understand what he means, but I don't want to say anything and sound like a dumb kid. What if he changes his mind about me being a *special needs* candidate? The thing is that Dr. Kerr—candid, extremely professional, and secure in what he's doing—can see right through my cover. He tries to explain it a little more clearly: "There can be a certain amount of feminization of the chest area in men, most specifically around the nipples. It can cause the growth of breast tissue. But again, those are rare cases, and we have another drug that counters it."

I don't blink. I just think to myself, *Okay, it's rare, and if I'm one of those few who do get it, there's another drug that'll prevent it.* With all of these benefits, what are a couple of *possible* side effects? It's like throwing a teenager the keys to a Ferrari and saying, "Oh, by the way, there's one problem with this car. It's goes really fucking fast, so be careful."

Dr. Kerr walks across the room and opens up his cupboard.

Inside are rows and rows of neatly stacked two-inch boxes. I feel a rush of excitement. *This is it,* I think—*those are the steroids and I'm finally going to get them.*

He returns with a couple of boxes. "This is Dianabol. You start off taking two of these a day—one in the morning and one with dinner. After two weeks, move up to three and stay there until you feel your gains aren't coming as fast. Then you can pop up to four a day."

He takes out a syringe. "I'll be giving you your first shot here in the office. After that, you can either have a friend do it or you can do it yourself." He instructs me to turn around and pull my pants down to expose my glutes. "When you give an injection, you want to divide the butt cheek into four quadrants by drawing an imaginary line down the center of it and another across it, as if you were drawing a cross. Just make sure you always shoot in the upper outside quadrant. Inject anywhere else and you might hit a nerve, which I promise will be extremely painful."

I've never been a big fan of needles. The last one I remember is a tetanus shot from stepping on a nail, and it hurt like shit. I watch closely as he fills the syringe with the oily substance.

"Does the needle have to be so big?"

"I have to make sure to get past the subcutaneous fat and into the muscle for the steroid to work." His voice is soothing and confident.

I nod. I'm getting my first shot of steroids and a rush of fear suddenly overcomes me. I'm scared. *Really* scared—not of the needle or the possible side effects.

I'm afraid that the steroids might not work.

Wrong again. The steroids don't just work, they are everything the doctor said they would be, and more. I'm surprised by how fast my body responds to the drugs. One day I'm benching 185, the next, 225. I get big, ripped, and strong, and I gain back all the weight I lost from the surgery, plus an additional ten pounds. I now weigh 220 and I'm quicker, stronger, and more explosive than ever before. Along with the weight comes a confidence and an aggression that I use on the football field to help destroy opposing players. I feel primal, like a lion—and the football field is my playground.

That's how steroids are. In the beginning, it's a honeymoon. You wonder how in the world you got so lucky to have found something so wonderful. In the beginning, they really are too good to be true.

I visit Dr. Kerr a few more times during the season. The goal is always to figure out how to get him to give me more and stronger drugs. Halfway through the season, I want to switch to another steroid called Anadrol. This drug is much stronger than Dianabol and is meant to be taken only once a day. It's the big daddy of all oral drugs—what the big boys take. Ever since Joe told me about Anadrol, I've secretly plotted to get on it because he says it gives him the greatest strength and weight gains, although its androgenic effects are a lot harder on the body. Joe coaches me, and when I see Kerr, I use the exact language Joe tells me to use. I say I've reached a plateau, I'm not getting gains, and I'm really not sure the steroids are working. Sure enough, I come home with the Anadrol and a warning to use it carefully.

On the field, I look strong and imposing in my uniform, but there's something else—something more than strength and speed. I have the unwavering belief that no one else on that field is as good as I am. I've always felt this way, but now I have the body and the aggression to back it up. When I was young, I would still get rattled when things went wrong. Now I feel unstoppable. When something goes wrong, the hurt and humiliation give way to violent anger.

During the season, I crush people on the field, making them pay each time they dare to run the ball my way. I make it a personal vendetta to punish offensive linemen who stand between the quarterback and me. By the time the season is over, I've corralled the MVP award and a football scholarship to San Jose State. My dream of getting out of Santa Ana has come true.

It's December and I've been on steroids for six months. When I ask Dr. Kerr if I should get off my cycle and stop taking the steroids for a while to give my body a rest, he says they're safe and I can stay on them indefinitely. After all, he has pro athletes and bodybuilders who've been on them for years without a break. But something instinctively tells me to go off the juice for a while. I don't want to abuse it, but more than that, I don't want to wear it out. I see steroids as a temporary thing, to help me recover from the injury. On the other hand, I don't want to lose the gains. But it's more than gains. I'm intoxicated by how it feels to be big, strong, and feared. I'm in love with my physical prowess and stature. Sadly, it fills up a lot of the empty spaces in me. So I sit in the doctor's office struggling with the decision. Finally, my *ego* makes a deal with my *soul*. I'll go off the steroids—but only for a little while.

Dr. Kerr gives me a bottle of human chorionic gonadotropin (HCG) to help me gently transition off my cycle. He says, "You need to take this to stimulate your testicles to produce testosterone naturally. It comes from the urine of pregnant women."

I keep thinking, *Pregnant woman's urine? I'm taking something from a pregnant woman's urine? What the hell? But he's the doctor,* I tell myself. I believe in him, I believe in medicine, and yet I know something is wrong—a feeling I choose to ignore. I'm determined to sweep anything that causes doubt under the carpet. My thoughts change from *I'm injecting something from a pregnant woman's piss* to what the drug is going to do for me.

The trouble is, no one prepared me for the difficulty of coming off steroids, when the body goes into a severe testosterone deficiency. I didn't realize that steroids made my body stop producing testosterone. It's as if the body says, "Hey, why should I make this stuff if you're going to be jamming it into me?" The larger the doses and longer the duration of steroid use, the greater the reduction of testosterone production. In fact, recent studies of Dianabol have shown that a conservative dosage of 20 mg leads to a 30 to 40 percent suppression of testosterone production after only ten days.

When I come off my cycle, I have only a fraction of the testosterone I had in my body before I started taking steroids. That means that all the positive effects of steroids vanish. If steroids are the chemical essence of manliness, physical power, and masculine aggression, when I go off, I swing to the polar opposite. I feel lethargic, I lose muscle mass, and my joints ache. The HCG helps alleviate these symptoms, but now I'm taking a drug to counter the effects of another drug. And again, it's made from a pregnant woman's piss.

I start injecting HCG twice a week as I taper off my regular drug cycle. Right away I notice a substantial change. I don't feel bad; I just don't feel fantastic, and the unbridled energy isn't there. I'm okay with it at first because the season has ended and I don't need that kind of energy. I see it as a time for my body to recuperate. Besides, I already have a scholarship. They can't take it away from me. Can they?

A week later the worst of the steroid crash hits me as I feel unmotivated, lethargic, with barely enough energy to get through the day. I don't even want to *think* about working out. When I try, I get depressed, not only because my gains have come to a screeching halt, but also, because I'm actually getting weaker. Even worse, I suddenly have problems with the girl I've been dating for the last six months.

In the beginning, steroids sent my sex drive through the roof. With the extra testosterone shooting through my system, I couldn't get enough sex—I couldn't scratch that itch. At eighteen, your hormones are already raging, and if you're a healthy, normal guy, your preoccupation with sex can be a bit daunting. Add artificial testosterone and it swings way out of control.

When I go off the steroids, it's a different story. I sneak over to my girlfriend's house in Garden Grove during the day while her mom is at work. We lie naked on her soft white sheets, the afternoon sun filtering in through her window as we kiss softly and rub our bodies against each other. Normally I'm ready quickly, but this time, nothing happens. I can't get my body to work. Finally I give up. I throw my legs over the side of the bed and sit there, head in my hands, completely frustrated and shocked. At this point I don't attribute my inability to perform to coming off the steroids. But the next time it occurs, I can no longer deny it.

It's weird when you're with a woman and you can't perform. It screws with both of your psyches. She smiles and tells me not to worry about it, but I can tell she thinks it's her fault, that I'm not attracted to her anymore. She sneaks off to the bathroom while I stand up and look at my naked body in the mirror. *Here I am,* I think, *with all of this muscle, a chiseled body, and I can't even be a man.*

I'd fooled myself into thinking that the drug was doing great things to my body and I was doing better than I really was. Now a thing like this happens and I know exactly where I stand. I have to admit that steroids have side effects, and it becomes an increasing struggle to have sex while I'm off my cycle. I have to accept it's no longer about sharing this intimate experience with a woman. Now it's about proving that I'm a man, proving that I can do it. I've begun to use sex purely for the sake of demonstrating that I'm virile. This is completely new to me—to have sex only to prove something. I don't realize that the body has a delicate hormonal cycle that I'm destroying. Even with all the evidence, I don't even consider getting off the juice for good. That simply is not an option. All I can think is *Shit, I better get back on the drugs.*

I stay off steroids for about six weeks, all the while feeling tremendous pressure to get back in shape. Junior college is like the minors. Now I'm going up to San Jose State and I want to be as big and ready as possible for the new season. All the players at a Division I college will be a lot stronger and faster. I'm determined not only to keep up with them. I want to be the best of the best.

With my mom, ecstatic after winning the MVP award
at Santa Ana JC.

CHAPTER 4

Go, Spartans

I hear the jarring pop of helmet against helmet, a jolting crack that sounds like a head-on car collision. A player lies unconscious on the practice field. The trainer runs out to the field, stands over the unconscious player, then waves for a stretcher.

This is during the spring game on my first visit San Jose State. I stand in stunned silence on the sidelines, in street clothes, along with all the other new recruits. *Holy shit! That was the hardest hit I've ever seen!*

They carry the player off the field on a stretcher. When he passes me, I see blood pouring out the side of his mouth. Welcome to Division I football. It's the early eighties and San Jose State's football program is on the upswing with its first top-twenty national ranking as well as having had two players chosen in the first round of the previous NFL draft.

My welcome to the downtown San Jose campus is quite different. I drove up in the evening. It didn't occur to me that I hadn't seen the campus in the daylight until the next morning, when I walked out of the dorm and stood in the harsh crack-of-dawn light, surveying the area. Shabby low-income houses line the litter-strewn streets. Up ahead, a small, battered Mexican restaurant sits with a crooked sign. This was before the Silicon Valley boom. San Jose State is "across the tracks," an area of town filled with minorities and college kids who are either local or can't get accepted anywhere else. Another rogues' gallery of misfits. Perfect. Just the way I like it.

A gray-haired, shabby-looking woman walks toward me on the sidewalk. She is homeless and her face is twisted in deep angst. She stops directly in front of me, lifts up her soiled skirt, squats down, and starts to pee. A yellow pool forms beneath her on the sidewalk, soaking her bare feet. After a long moment, she abruptly stands up, walks off, and disappears down an alley. Her pee-stained footprints trailed behind her, the only evidence she was there. It's a sobering experience, but the truth is, I don't care.

I chose San Jose State because it's close to home and because Bobby Frasco, the quarterback during my freshman year at Santa Ana, is now the quarterback at San Jose. I chose San Jose because of the football program's rapid rise to prominence. And mostly I chose San Jose State because *they* chose me.

When I arrive, I'm pushing 235 pounds, ripped and hard. I can see the oohs and aahs in the coaches' eyes when they first see me. The coach I want to impress most is Claude Gilbert. He recruited me—he believes in me. Coach Gilbert stands five-nine, but he's an imposing figure with his dark, intense eyes and legendary temper. He demands respect; you want to work hard to please him. In the three and a half years I played for him, I only heard him tell one joke, and it was at my expense, when I showed up in bright red Reebok high-tops for our first spring film session.

Coach Gilbert took one look at them and said, "Clark, I wish I had me two pair of those shoes. One to shit on, the other to cover them up with."

The night after the spring game I can't sleep. My heart beats wildly in my chest as the sound of the hit reverberates through my head. I can't get the vision of the guy lying knocked out on the field out of my head. I roll over and look at my watch. It blinks back—6 a.m. I roll out of bed and head to the gym.

Although I'm on a scholarship, I know I still have plenty of learning to do, and the next three and a half years will be a constant battle. Gains will come in increments that *might* separate me from the other scholarship athletes. There's a science to getting even better that the avid fan rarely comprehends—countless hours in the gym, endless film sessions, along with day after day of being on the field in the pounding sun. The difference between being a starter and an all-American is measured by fractions of a second.

To say I "work out" is an understatement. In the gym, driven by the fear of failure, the fear of not being good enough—fast enough, not being able to hit people hard enough—I give blood, birthing this new body through sweat and hard work. Dr. Kerr tells me steroids allow you to work out harder because they help you recover more quickly. I put his theory to the test and don't miss a workout from the day of the spring game until the first day of summer practice at San Jose State.

I never feel I'm compromising my morality to get ahead. You have to remember, this is 1982. Steroids won't become illegal to sell in America until 1988 and won't be illegal to possess until 1990. I never look at steroids as giving me an unfair advantage. They're a daily part of my life, like taking a shit after my morning cup of coffee.

But with my body, it's a different story.

I know somewhere deep inside I'm giving pieces of it away, paying for my gains with a pound of flesh. But this Faustian bargain isn't something athletes want to deal with. We don't want to know. We're in the business of denial and self-abuse. Our bodies are commodities, our mode of trade. We're used to pain. We feel it with each snap of the ball, each collision, and we're taught "Don't quit. Don't give in to the pain." So when you get the inkling that something is wrong, you *do not* give in, you *do not* quit. So my steroid routine remains the same as it was with Dr. Kerr. At this point I'm always careful to stay pretty much within the prescription limits—four to six Dianabol a day, along with 2 cc of testosterone twice a week.

Today is the first day of practice for the season. I wake up that morning with a fire in my gut. An intensity. A sense of purpose. After a summer of insane training, I'm confident I'll succeed at this level. More than confident. I'm sure. The best way to show off my summer training is to bust out a blistering time in the forty-yard dash—the measuring stick for speed in football. I'm so confident and anxious, I don't even stretch before I kneel down into a sprinter's stance next to the orange cone on the starting line. The whistle blows and I explode off the line, every muscle working in sleek and perfect unison, hurtling me along as I burst ahead of the guy next to me. The world zips by me in frenzy. This is going to be my best-for-forty time ever.

Bang! White flares of lightning blast through my head as a mind-numbing pain explodes through the back of my leg. My body spasms, my back arches, my head and arms fly back dramatically, like a soldier shot in the back in a war movie. I stagger, then lumber to the ground like a giant primate taken down by a single shot from a hunter.

Oddly enough, lying there on the ground, I think about a *National Geographic* special on hunting the forbidding beasts of the jungle. The narrator's pompous, English-accented voice suddenly starts to play in my head: "The lion is king of the jungle, who strikes fear in all, except for one blood-hungry insatiable beast"—a dramatic pause—"man." Then footage plays of a hunter shooting—murdering a lioness in front of her cubs. The cubs scream in a way that sounds eerily human. The narrator continued, "Man, Homo sapiens, the only beast who kills for pleasure."

I'm struck by the pure savagery of it, just as I'm struck by the savagery of the players that hover over me. I can read their minds. A part of them is upset that I'm hurt . . . the other part is *happy*. It means one less player to compete against.

Back in the training room, the trainer digs his finger into a gap in the muscle of the back of my thigh. "Do you feel this right here?"

I nod.

"You've torn your hamstring."

"You mean pulled it," I correct him.

"No, you've *torn* it. Ripped the muscle in half. You can't repair it. You can only strengthen the muscles around it to compensate for the tear."

"How long will I be out?" I ask, gripped with fear.

"At least six to eight weeks. But it's going to get worse before it gets better."

My face turns ashen. In that moment I see my name erased from the Wall of Fame. It will no longer glitter on that square plaque where the names of the best are inscribed. My dream is dying again.

The next day I'm on crutches, and my entire leg, from the bottom of my glute all the way down to my toes, is black-and-blue. Coach Gilbert tells me he's going to redshirt me—meaning I have to sit the year out. I'm disappointed beyond belief. But I'll have a chance to fully heal my hamstring and learn the defensive schemes. Plus, I won't lose a year of eligibility and I'll be getting a free year of school.

As soon I can, I attack my rehabilitation like a madman. The trainer and I become best friends and I become a student of the body. I want to know everything about how this magnificent organ called the human body functions. I spend hours, with an assist from my roommate Frank, devouring books on anatomy, physiology, kinesiology, nutrition, applied biology—whatever I can get my hands on.

Before this, I only read enough to get by in school and stay eligible. Now I feel like a premed student. I can tell you where your quadratus laborum inserts and attaches and what its function is. I can tell you about the macromolecule ATP and the energy currency to the cell. But mainly I want to know why this body I built with such care and precision is betraying me.

The answer I come up to one I don't want to believe.

Steroids.

My muscles grew too fast too quickly, and the connective tissue in the muscle didn't have a chance to catch up and hold the new strength. When I exploded off the line and sprinted, I put insane demand on a young muscle that wasn't strong enough to handle it. It's similar to what happens when you take a rubber band and violently pull at it until it snaps. Only this isn't a rubber band. It's my hamstring and I realize that the magic wand that helped me recover from a knee injury and get to San Jose is also the culprit that is taking my opportunity away. Steroids are a double-edged sword, one I would throw myself on over and over, until I couldn't feel a thing.

I spend the season on the sidelines watching as it moves excruciatingly slowly. I feel like damaged goods, like a banana that lost its peel and is left out to rot.

Let me come out and say that no coach, as far as I know, ever gave a player steroids at San Jose State. There isn't a jar in the training room filled with 'roids. But the competition is fierce and the stakes are high. You succeed here and you have a pretty good shot at making it in the high-paying, glorified world of professional football. That pat on the ass by the coach as he passed by saying, "You're looking a little thin," always meant more to me than "Have an extra serving of mashed potatoes at the training table." There was always the implied whisper of "I don't care what you do, but do whatever it takes to put some size on."

It's up to each individual to decide what he's willing and needs to do to try to breathe in the rarefied air of the NFL. But when you see people around you exploding with strength and size gains, it's almost impossible not to indulge to keep up and compete.

After ten months of vicious rehab, I come back the next year and I am "the guy." I am tied for the lead in the conference with quarterback sacks, and I play perhaps the most inspired minutes of my life against Fresno State, where I have four sacks alone and am named the conference's most valuable player.

NFL scouts know my name. My life is everything I've dreamed about. It's like a marvelous present finally being unwrapped. You see, to me, playing is not what it's about. Any asshole can play. I want to lead the conference in tackles. I want my name in *Sports Illustrated*. I want sportscasters to gush about me.

The next season I'm on the cover of the media guide, and Coach Gilbert designs the entire defense around me. It's called an eagle defense and I'm the "enforcer." The idea is to line me up against the weakside offensive tackle, the tackle without the tight end. At the snap of the ball, I'd burst off the line into the backfield creating such havoc it would disrupt the entire offense. Like a rogue car on the freeway going 110 mph in the wrong direction, I'm looking to create collisions and concussions. The scheme works perfectly in practice, and I'm looking forward to my senior year at SJSU like no other.

The first game of the year is against the California Bears at Berkeley in front of forty-five thousand people. Cal is in the Pac Ten, arguably the toughest conference in college football. These are the games I salivate over—a measuring stick of my ability.

In the first quarter on the second series of plays, under the sweltering summer sun, I reinjure my hamstring. I'm shocked, horrified, but I shouldn't be surprised. I am bigger than ever this year, trying to keep up with the even bigger demands and expectations. And my hamstring just isn't strong enough to withstand the torque. The rest of the season is a struggle at best. The Spartans stumble badly. I feel that it's all my fault. But there's nothing I can do to get better—nothing will make this nightmare go away. Whenever I get in, I throw my body around recklessly with no thought of personal safety. It's as if I'm frantically trying, in a single play, to make up for an entire season that I know is slipping away.

As the season progresses, I squeeze harder, driving my body as far as I can. But like a palm full of sand, the harder I squeeze, the more it slips through my fingers. I feel like a voyeur, looking in on a world that no longer has a place for me.

The brightest moment of my senior year is against Stanford. On fourth down, I slip through Stanford's offensive line and crush their quarterback. Ignited by the hit, the crowd of seventy thousand explodes onto their feet and screams my name. But I'm deadened to the roar and the pandemonium that surrounds me, immune to it, unable to feel it.

Here, I realize that *maybe* something is wrong with chasing the hollow dream of fame and adulation. I mean, seventy thousand people are screaming my name—and *I don't feel a thing*. Perhaps I know that truth, that the light blazes its brightest for only fleeting seconds, that this moment is only temporary.

A Thursday-night game on ESPN against Long Beach State is the final game of the season. I play my heart and soul out as the whistles of the officials, the yells of the coaches, the sounds of the game, surround me. I grope for moments and feelings that could've been. Cleats stuck in the clumpy sod, I stand on the sidelines and watch as the stadium clock runs out. For the last ten years, my universe has existed inside one hundred yards. As the clock hits zero, I realize once again that I have absolutely no idea what to do with my life.

All I know is that I have to get out of San Jose. I'm haunted by thoughts of letting down my teammates, my coach, and myself. I feel the entire weight of the disappointing season on my shoulders. Sure, injuries happen in football. Everyone knows it's part of the game. But I still can't shake the horrible feeling of how I let them down. When Gilbert recruited me, there was an unspoken agreement. "I'm going to choose you and you're going to bust your ass and give me everything you've got." He lived up to his part of the agreement. I didn't live up to mine. And it really hurts. I hate myself.

I'm number 48. I was supposed to be
the man this season.

Becoming an Expert

I t's hard to imagine a life without football, but the game seems to be moving on without me. I'm drifting, trying to piece my life back together after a disappointing finish to my college football career, and land back at my father's house in Santa Ana. I think of it as a temporary stop—just until I get into camp somewhere and show a team what I can do. But no one is calling or inviting me to a training camp. I can't even land an agent.

It's all hard to fathom. Just a few months ago, I was playing in front of seventy thousand people. Now I'm back in my high school bedroom, staring at the sailor-themed wallpaper while my dreams plunge so fast, I can't hold on to them anymore. All the plaques and trophies on my Wall of Fame, with my once-glittering name etched across them, now seem like timeworn relics in a pharaoh's tomb.

I close my eyes and try to remember—try to keep the memories alive. For a brief moment I can smell the pungent grass odor drifting through the air and hear the stadium come alive with thunderous applause. Then it's gone and another memory, like an unwelcome friend, comes thundering in.

I'm fifteen years old—the night my dad made a coward out of me when I walked in on him hitting my stepmother. I can still see the look on her red-cheeked, tearstained face as she cowers in the corner of the living room like a scared animal. But when our eyes meet, the look on her face *isn't* fear. It's the look of shame and humiliation of a woman who gets beaten and *chooses* to stay. I have the same look on my face when I turn and walk up the stairs without saying a word. I wish I were man enough at fifteen to run over and throw my father against the wall and ask him what the hell he thinks he's doing. Then pick up my battered stepmom and take her firmly by the shoulders and tell her not to *ever* let him do that again.

But I don't. I'm terrified of my father. I am a coward. And that is something I have to live with every day of my life. Maybe that's why a sense of right and wrong burns so brightly in me now, and why I'm deeply moved by blind courage. Back then, though, the next morning I go to the track to rid myself of the lingering memories. I run as hard as I can, until my heart rattles against my ribs and my lungs burst, and then I'm cleansed, baptized by the fire and adrenaline that only a hard workout can bring.

I had a complex relationship with my father. I loved and feared him when I was young. I idolized him as a teen. I was pissed off at him and resented him as a man. And I missed the hell out of him when he was gone because, if you wanted to see a real fan, if you wanted to see someone who cared about my career as if it were his own, then you should have seen my dad. From the moment I started to excel and a crowd gathered to see me play, he was in the stands maniacally cheering, his deep, gravelly voice rising above all others: "That's my son!"

Sometimes it seemed that he got even more satisfaction than I did from a great play. When my star shone brightest, it gleamed on him. He lived vicariously through me, disguised as my biggest fan.

CHAPTER 5

I think it filled a gaping crevice in the fabric of who he was. The thing we never spoke about.

My brother.

When my father struggled, clawed, and bled to get us off welfare, I realized he was a tough son of a bitch, but he also oozed charisma. He'd shake your hand, look you in the eye with his baby blues, and make you feel like the most important person in the world. But, if you crossed him, he'd smack you in the mouth. That's just the way it was. And, yep, he drank.

I push these thoughts out of my head and focus on the positive things in life. I've got a new drug dealer. Fuck Kerr, I'm going to be getting it right from the source. I tell myself I'm tired of making the grueling drive up to his office, tired of the extra fees, tired of the blood test, tired of the exams. But the truth is, I'm tired of Kerr giving me only a limited supply. And I think I know more than he does.

That's how it is with steroids. You quickly become an "expert" and you trust the information from the guys in the trenches taking the gear, not some doc in a smock. Little do I know that Dr. Kerr has been doing exactly the right thing with me—ordering blood tests and prescribing limited dosages.

I pull into the parking lot of the strip mall on a spit of land near the beach. I hop out of my jeep and walk toward a beige brick building with warped lettering that reads PHARMACY without the P. HARMACY broods at me like a crooked frown. Inside, platinum-haired seniors wait in line for their monthly doses of life. As I duck under the counter, a sour-faced senior cracks, "Hey, you can't go back there!"

I flash a toothy smile at her. "I just did."

Her face contorts as I disappear down the aisle.

That's where I find Peter. A fifty-year-old, impossibly skinny man, who looks like a skeleton covered with a thin sheet of skin.

He is the owner. He is my new drug dealer. He is my dad's best friend.

"What can I get you, Dan?"

"Can I have anything I want?"

"*Anything,*" he says with a hippie, peace, love, I-want-to-share-my-drugs-with-you smile. He leads me to an aisle with wall-to-wall drugs from floor to ceiling. My face lights up like a kid's on Christmas morning.

"There," I say, pointing to the boxes of testosterone.

"Cypionate or propionate?" he asks.

"Both."

"Aren't they the same?"

"Oh, no, no, no, my dear friend," I inform him, "there is a huge but subtle difference. Cypionate is oil-based. It stays in your system longer, but it also causes water retention. Propionate is water-based and is quicker-acting. I like to take a little of both because I feel the prop' quicker, but I like the way the cyp' sits with me longer, but I'm not a fan of the water retention. If I take more than a cc of cypionate twice a week, I'll actually hold an extra five pounds of water, and it causes me to cramp up in my calves after sprints, so I like to balance it out with the propionate."

He looks at me, incredulous.

"Oh, and I'd love to get two bottles of the 2.5-milligram Anavar. Summer's coming and I want to cut up a little bit so I look ripped for the beach. And don't forget the syringes. Twenty-one gauge, inch and a half."

Peter smiles. "Looks like you did your homework."

"I am my own science project."

"Anything else?"

"You gotta bottle of HCG? I think my estrogen count is a little high. My left nipple is a little sore. It might be aromatizing."

It's actually more than a little sore and I have recently noticed a hard growth around the nipple area that's tender to the touch. I'm horrified, but I figure it'll go away with a few doses of HCG.

Peter disappears down an aisle, then returns a few moments later with a vial of HCG. He hands me the vial and shows me a blue-and-white pill in his hand. "You ever try these?" he asks with a crooked grin.

"What are they?"

"I call it a combo. It's the same high you get from heroin without the addictive qualities."

I suddenly see Peter for who he really is. A junkie in a white smock who figured out how to get his illegal drugs legally.

"No thanks, man," I tell him, "I'm not into that shit."

"You sure? They're your dad's favorite."

I feel like I've just been punched in my stomach. I know Dad drinks too much, but I don't know about this. I want to take the bag of 'roids and shove them up Peter's ass and tell him to fuck off. But I don't. Because I need the drugs.

While I'm waiting, hopefully, to get picked up by a team, I get a job bouncing at an eighteen-and-over club. The first thing the owner, Matt, says when he hires me is "Don't fight. That's the number one rule here."

I nod.

Then Matt leans in with a devilish grin. "But if you do have to fight or take someone down, just don't leave any marks. That way they won't be able to press charges." Matt is big, 280 pounds, but he's soft and can't fight, which is why he brings me in to cover the door at a new nightclub called the Roaring 20's in Orange County.

This is where I first meet Theresa. She is clearly older than the other girls standing in line, but she doesn't seem to mind. At thirty, she thinks she has what it takes to give the eighteen-year-old girls a run for their money.

"Hi," I say as all five feet two inches of her stands in front of me, fishing her ID out of her wallet. She looks great, but there's something else about her . . . a quality I can't quite put my finger on. She reaches up for her ID and I hold on to it. Our eyes meet. I see a melancholy, a lingering sadness behind her veil of a smile—but I also see an intense desire to please, that she's the kind of girl who would do anything sexually. I'm not talking about a freak. That's something completely different. I'm not interested in a girl with a treasure chest of sex toys who needs three different kinds of vibrators to cum or a girl who wants you to smack her around or something crazy like that.

A quality in Theresa suggests she's been hurt and finds solace in serving and pleasing a man—that she wants to be held tight and told that everything is going to be okay.

I take her home that night, we get lost in each other, and for a brief moment it takes us away from the world. But I'm wrong about Theresa. She is running while standing still. Running away from a dark, damaged part of her that can never be touched. It's an ugliness and a thirst that all the reassurance in the world can't quench. She has tried to excise it over the years with too many trips to the plastic surgeon, in search of the beauty she can't find inside.

I continue to see Theresa as I get through the first handful of nights at the club without an altercation. A few harsh words and the threat of violence is usually enough to handle any situation. But there's always someone who wants to test you. Someone who's trying to be a hero.

It happens during my second week at the club when I'm working the floor. As I walk casually through the crowd, checking out the tanned Southern California trust-fund kids, out of the corner of my eye I see two college guys squaring off with each other, a small crowd starting to form around them. I cross the room and step between them.

"Whoa, whoa, fellas," I say. "Let's just take it easy and chill. There's a lot of good times to be had tonight. No one wins, no one loses. Just walk off and have a good time."

One of the combatants, the smart one, knows a good idea when he hears it and immediately deflates. "I'm cool, man," he says.

The other guy, with the upturned collar, looks at me, his face filled with righteous indignation, and says, "Look, this is none of your business. Why don't you fuck off."

I feel the rage, the adrenaline dump shoots through my veins, but on the outside, not a ripple. I look at him calmly and say, "There's no need to use that kind of language. I'm going to have to ask you to leave." I put a hand lightly on the back of his shoulder and gesture toward the exit.

"Get your hands off of me!" he shouts, shoving my hand away.

My hands involuntarily clench into fists. *I will kill you, motherfucker. I will fucking kill you.* His chin blinks like a neon sign that says, "Hit me." I feel my body turn to position itself to throw a left hook. It'll be quick and beautiful, he'll never see it coming. After he drops, I'm going to stomp the shit out of his face. But then I hear Matt's voice warning me, "Don't leave any marks."

I hesitate. He mistakenly sees this as weakness and becomes bolder. He looks to his buddies: chest puffed out, like he'd just won something, then turns to me and says, "Now, get the fuck away from me."

I smile—because I know I'm going to hurt him and I'm going to enjoy it. I let him revel in his glory for an instant longer—until my hands explode outward and grab his neck. In one swift move, I lift him off the ground and drive him back, slamming him into the wall. I hear the air buffeting out of him since I have him suspended off the ground, pinned against the wall, choking the life out of him. His face turns sheet white as he furiously tries to suck in air. Instinctively, both of his hands shoot up and grab mine as his legs kick and sputter.

I lean in close. "Say something now. Come on, say something now!"

He tries to speak. All he can manage is a raspy grunt.

"I can't hear you." I smash the back of his head against the wall. "You're leaving. Are we clear?"

He nods and squeaks out a yes. I slam his head against the wall again just for good measure and release my death grip. He drops to the ground like a sack of shit. Matt rushes over, feral excitement in his eyes. "Hey, I'm sorry, Matt, I kinda lost my temper."

Matt's face gleams with excitement. "Dude, that was awesome." He smacks me on the back and says, "And best of all, you didn't leave any marks." The other bouncers come over, throw the guy out, and treat me like I'm some kind of hero, awed by my choke-and-lift technique.

I need air. I step outside and look down at my hands. They are still trembling. I don't feel like a hero. I feel swollen. Swollen with disease. I'm stunned at how quick the rage overtook me. I'm scared and awed by its power. It feels bigger than I am. It feels alive inside me.

It is now fall. I've been living with Theresa for the last three months, and one morning she walks into the bedroom and announces, "I'm pregnant."

I sit up in bed in utter disbelief. "But, T, you told me it was safe—that you didn't even ovulate—that there was no possible way you could get pregnant."

"It's a miracle of God."

I lie there staring at her, stunned. I can't believe she's trying to pull this religious bullshit on me. Not only is she not religious, I don't think she's ever been in a church. She must really think I'm an idiot.

"Come on, T. Like I'm supposed to believe that bullshit!"

"Either that . . . or you've got really strong sperm," she coos. The words hang in the air.

Really strong sperm? Oh, well, why didn't she just come out and say that? That I can buy, even though it makes no fucking sense. You don't ovulate so there's no egg dropping down into the fallopian tube, but my sperm is so macho, fierce, and strong that it bravely swims up the canal, kicks the living shit out of whatever is in its way, then rips out a hostage egg from the ovaries, then infiltrates and impregnates it.

Yeah, that could happen. Well, at least in my mind anyway.

I am twenty-two. She is thirty and *way* smarter. Okay, maybe *smarter* isn't the right word. Hell, let's just call it like it is. She is a damn liar. And I am an idiot.

"But, Theresa, I can't be saddled down with a kid," I protest. "I'm trying to get with a team and could end up anywhere in America."

She looks me square in the eye. "I don't need anything from you. If you haven't noticed, you're staying at my house. I have my own money, my own things." She pauses for a second and feels prompted to repeat, "I don't need anything from you."

She has a point. I *am* living with her in her plush pad with a pool at the bottom of the Tustin foothills. She drives a convertible Mercedes, has her own skis and a bowling ball with her name on it.

"Okay." I shrug. "Just don't tell my dad. Let me tell him when I'm ready."

She nods in agreement and leaves the room.

An hour later the phone rings. It's my father. "Why didn't you tell me Theresa was pregnant?"

I'm too dumbfounded to respond. All I can manage is "Huh?"

"I said, why didn't you tell me Theresa was pregnant?"

"What . . . what makes you say that?"

"She called me a few minutes ago and said, 'Hi, *Grandpa*.'"

Fall quickly turns to winter. I'm still staying with Theresa and bouncing at the bar, but I'm having a hard time controlling my temper. I'm filled with unbridled rage. It's with me every step I take. I search my mind for an answer as to why. It could be the baby that I'm not ready for with a woman I don't want to spend the rest of my life with. Maybe my rage stems from the disappointment of not getting on a team and helplessly watching a dream unravel. But when the answer finally comes to me, I realize it's been tapping at my door for the last five years.

Steroids. With football, there was an outlet for the rage. Now, there's nothing. I train, but it's not enough . . . to rid myself of this walking anger like fire. I think for the first time maybe I should just flat out quit steroids. But I won't allow myself that luxury. I need to be ready—in case a team calls.

At the club, my choke-and-lift technique is becoming a nightly habit. Matt is looking at me differently. What was once "awesome" is now a liability. After a couple of threatened lawsuits, I know I have to get out of there, but I have no place to go. And my life with Theresa is a nightmare. She's squeezing me, trying to make me into the man she wants me to be. She's talking about my going back to finish school and us raising a kid. But I want nothing to do with the web she's spinning. A part of me feels like I'm still a kid, trying to find my place in the world. If I don't know what *I'm* doing, how in the hell can I tell a kid anything worthwhile?

Each day I feel more and more suffocated until I literally cannot breathe. I sit on Theresa's balcony one evening under the glow of the warm Southern California sunset, so consumed with the pressures I can't see straight. I remind myself to breathe. I take a good long inhale and feel the stirring of dreams in my stomach. I know I'm not done. I know something good is going to happen. I just have no idea what.

That night, I get a call from a friend, Bobby Frasco. He's been in Italy playing American football since he left San Jose State the year before. He wants to meet me for breakfast.

CHAPTER 6

I'm 260 and Pounding Pasta

"You ever fuck a transsexual?" Bobby asks me, chewing on his eggs Benedict.

"What? Me? Hell no," I stammer.

"Then don't come to Milan," he says with a grin.

"They're really playing American football in Italy?" I have to ask because when I think of Italy, two things that never come to mind are transsexuals or American football.

"Yep. They've been playing it for about ten years. It's a far cry from the NFL, but they pay you a weekly salary, put you up in a hotel, and cover all your meals."

"How much salary?"

"About a grand a week, plus all expenses."

"Who do you play against?"

Bobby talks to me about teams and divisions and how each team is only allowed three Americans on their roster. I push the eggs around my plate. "Does anyone show up for the games?"

"About a thousand people. But I'll be honest with you. The conditions aren't great. We play on an old soccer field, the skill level is equivalent to junior college and there's no broadcast-TV support. Soccer rules over there. The football team is a hobby for a rich guy—and the Italian players don't get paid. They play because they're crazy about American football. But last year, at the Italian Super Bowl, we had nearly twenty thousand people."

"Any NFL players over there?"

"Not really. Mostly guys from smaller schools who love the game and still want to play. I told them about you and they're ready to sign you, if you're interested."

"Milan, huh?"

"All you need to know is it's the female-modeling capital of the world," he teases.

My eyes light up.

"If you're into it, we need to move fast. The season is about to start and we're desperate for another American player."

"When do you need my answer?"

"By the time breakfast is over," Bobby says with a smile.

I take a good look at the rising sun, turn to Bobby, and ask, "How do you say D-bol in Italian?"

Two days later I'm on a plane to Milan. I sit across from Bobby as he explains the defensive scheme. "We'll be running a six-one defense. You'll be the middle linebacker. It's designed to stop the run because most teams don't pass well. And be prepared to coach—you're the d-line and the linebackers' coach."

"Player coach?" I nodded that I could handle it.

"We play our games on Saturday and only practice Tuesday and Thursday at seven p.m. The other guys have to work during the day. One guy is a dentist. We got a cop, a lawyer, a plumber, a mechanic, a doctor, a gym owner, and a couple of players right out of college."

Great. I smirk. Another rogues' gallery of misfits.

Bebo, the head coach, picks us up at the airport. Dressed in jeans, Ray-Bans, and a short-sleeved polo shirt with an upturned collar, he looks like anything but a head coach. He whisks us straight to the practice field, where Bebo parades me in front of my new team-mates like I'm his prom date. The players whoop and holler and examine me like I'm a prize stallion who just won the Kentucky Derby. A couple of guys walk up, kiss me on the cheeks, and hug me like I'm their savior. Others squeeze my biceps and huge quads and let out gasps of "Ooh" and "Aah."

They keep saying how honored they are to have a huge college star playing for them. I'm uncomfortable with the adulation because it isn't true. "Guys, I wasn't exactly a big—"

A player cuts me off. "What-a you talking about?" He speaks English in a thick Italian accent. "In Fresno State you had a four sacks, eight tackles, and a fumble recovery." The other players roar their approval. I glance at Bobby. He shrugs his shoulders and smiles. Another player blurts out, "There's no way we can't win the Super Bowl with you." Then, like a bunch of rowdy frat boys, they all begin to chant, "Super Bowl! Super Bowl! Super Bowl!" I have to admit, it feels damn good. You see, in college, at 240 pounds, I was an average-size player. Here, I'm the largest player on the team. A freak show. But in my mind, I'm not nearly big enough. I can never be big enough.

As I settle into life in Italy, we're not living in the bustling met-ropolitan city of Milan like Bobby promised. Instead, we are staying in a small town called Novara, a twenty-minute train ride from Milan. During an early-morning walk, I quickly discover that Bobby, another American player called Desmond, and I are the only English-speaking people in the town besides our coach. I'm disappointed when I see my new living quarters—a gloomy three-story building no nicer than the apartment I shared with my sister and roommate, Bill, during my senior year in college. At least there is biweekly maid service. I'm also disappointed to learn there are only three TV sta-tions, and none of the broadcasts are in English. Ditto for the radio.

The good news? My room is right above one of the best restaurants in Novara—a four-star culinary gem. Part of our contract stipulates that we have an open tab at the restaurant. So, here I'm introduced to a whole new world of food: carpaccio, veal scaloppini, prosciutto.

"You're sure you can buy it right over the counter?" I ask Bobby as we enter the pharmacy.

"Yep," he answers as we approach the pharmacist. He rattles something off to her in Italian. After a long conversation, the pharmacist disappears down an aisle and returns with a small box that she hands to Bobby. "She says this is just like D-bol."

"Are you sure it's real?" I ask.

"Yep, it's regulated by the government."

I study the box and figure if they can make a Ferrari and Armani, they can probably make steroids. I get a bottle of D-bol and a couple of bottles of testosterone along with a cutting drug called Finajet—a water-based steroid used to get ripped, but it has to be shot almost every day.

Now that I have my juice, I'm taking it upon myself to teach English to some of the pretty women in town. Sipping coffee with Bobby and a couple of local girls, I point to different parts of my face and teach them the English word for eyes . . . ears . . . nose . . . and when I point to my mouth, I say, "Penis."

They point to their own mouths and repeat, "Penis."

I do it over and over, and each time it makes Bobby and me crack up. And each time Bebo, who is from this town, buries his head in his hands and says, "Oh, *mamma mia*." Obviously, this childlike behavior is not going to get me any female companionship, so for the first few weeks I spend every night alone watching one of three Italian television channels.

The only thing left to do is to read, and I have to say that books are opening up a whole new world to me. I haven't really cracked a book since high school, and I like the way they shut out the world and take me away. I start with books I should have read in school like *Catcher in the Rye*, *The Great Gatsby*, and *I Know Why the Caged Bird Sings*. They become my refuge and my escape. In the meantime, I play football with Desmond, Mauro, Gianni, Francesco, and Bebo. They are maniacs, rebels who shun the Italian national pastime, soccer, and know and love everything about American football. With all of our skills and passions combined, we easily win our first three games, quickly becoming the team to beat.

I'm learning that the guys on my team are like guys on any team. They love to play hard, drink, party, and tell stories about their hard-fought battles on the field, over and over. Kissing each other on the cheeks all the time is a little weird, but I'm getting used to it. One custom I'll never get used to, though, is the Italian fascination with transsexuals.

The first night we go out in Milan to get laid, we end up at a giant warehouse of blinking lights—a club called Hollywood, where all the models supposedly hang out. I have a couple of beers and am making my way around the club, checking out the scene, when I spot an amazing-looking girl in a skintight outfit, dancing by herself. She's maybe five feet two inches, and has a slamming little body with a tight waist and ample breasts.

I point her out to one of my Italian buddies. "There. I like her."

He shakes a finger at me. "That's a guy."

"Get outta here! There's no way that chick is a guy."

"I promise you, Dan. She used to be a man. But maybe you're into that kind of thing—"

No, no, no! Not only am I *not* into that kind of thing, I have never even seen a transsexual outside sex-ed class. And that she-male looked nothing like the one here, shaking her ass on the dance floor. I later learn that more than a few Italian men like transsexuals. It's the ultimate taboo, and they're willing to pay good money to have sex with them. Most of the trannies are small-framed, young gay men from Brazil who save up their money, come to Italy, get the operation, and make a good living selling their bodies to Italian men.

Now, let me tell you about Paula. Easily the most famous transsexual in Italy, she is an intoxicatingly sexy model whose face graces countless covers of fashion magazincs. I have a few encounters with Paula when she's hanging out at a hot nightclub, Amnazi, dressed only in garters, fuck-me pumps, and a lace bra. Paula isn't bashful. She'll bend over and show her goods, as if to say, "See, it looks just like the real thing, tastes like the real thing. You should try it. You'll like it!" Paula loves to have sex with Americans and will tell you flat out she wants to fuck you.

"Voglio scopare," she'll say in a gravelly male voice.

"I want nothing to do with you," I say back to her. But I do have to admit that I once took a peak at Paula's womanhood. And, yep, it looked like the real thing.

I'm getting used to being in Italy, I like it, and now, one sultry Saturday afternoon, I stand dwarfed in the shadows against the massive flanks of Milan's magnificent Duomo cathedral, which took five centuries to build. Here I get word from Gianni, a bodybuilder who owns a local gym in the city, that you can buy Parabolin—the Holy Grail of steroids—over the counter in Switzerland. The word on the street is that it will incinerate fat while packing on pounds of thick muscle, with no water retention. In the States, it's hard to find and expensive at twenty bucks a shot. In Switzerland it's two bucks a vial and as easy to find as aspirin.

When I first get my hands on Parabolin, it's love at first shot. The drug really grabs me, almost like a sexual experience. It comes in a sleek, two-inch glass ampoule that carries a single dose. I'm intoxicated by the cool touch of the glass ampoule and the golden hue of the oil it contains. I'll never forget the pneumatic pop as I snap off the head of the vial. I bring it to my nose and take a deep whiff, the musky oil invading my nostrils. Once I inject it, I can feel the drug surge through my body, and I actually taste the musky oil in my mouth. It gives me a need and an instant sense of gratification as the tiny oily atoms of the drug grab me.

On the field, it seems like all we can do is win. And with each game, I feel increased pressure to perform, to take the team on my shoulders and carry them to a championship. Maybe it's a way to make up for my failures at San Jose.

After ten games we are still undefeated and are favorites to win the all-important Super Bowl. I know the Parabolln is working. I just don't know how well—until I hop on the bench press and throw up four hundred pounds like it's nothing. I'm amazed. Normally, even on the juice, I struggle for reps at four hundred pounds. Breathless with excitement, I look at Bobby and say, "Let's slap on another fifty pounds." Bobby obliges. Four hundred and fifty pounds are now on the bar. I've never lifted this much weight before. I lay it on the bench, yank the weight off, and throw it up for five reps.

"Shit!" Bobby says. "You're an animal."

"Bob, throw another fifty pounds."

He looks at me for a quick beat. Then he slides two twenty-five-pound plates on. He doesn't want to mention how much weight is on the bar, kind of like when a pitcher is going into the ninth inning with a no-hitter, you shut up and leave him the hell alone. But I know exactly how much weight is on the bar—five hundred pounds.

I dip my hands in the chalk and smack them together. A white puff of dust rises into the air. I lie back on the bench, take a few deep breaths, and lock my hands around the bar. With a mighty grunt, I jerk the weight off the rack. The plates on each side clang together as the bar buckles. As I strain to balance the weight, a bolt of pain shoots through my shoulders. A wave of panic sweeps over me. Shit, I put too much weight on. I slowly lower the bar to my chest. Every vein in my body explodes as I drive the weight up. It stalls halfway up, my tendons and muscles screaming. Bobby moves in to help me.

"Don't touch it!" I yell. With one mighty surge, I drive the weight all the way up. But instead of racking it, I drop the five hundred pounds back down to my chest and press it back up. I throw the weight on the rack, jump to my feet and scream, "Arrgghhhh!"

"Jesus! That was awesome!" Bobby stares at me for a long moment, his mouth agape. "You're freakin' huge!"

I take a look in the mirror. He's right. My chest looks like mountains of beef, and my arms are impossibly thick and striated.

"How much do you weigh?" he asks.

"I don't know. I haven't weighed myself in a while."

Bobby and I move over to the scale—one of those old, mechanical, black-and-white scales with the balance-beam arm. I hop on and lock the little black counterweight on the horizontal bar at 200 pounds. Bobby starts sliding the little meter across . . . 220 . . . 230 . . . 240 . . . all the way to the end . . . 250. We wait for the little arm to move down and settle in the middle of the bracket. It doesn't budge.

"What's the most you've ever weighed?" Bobby asks.

"Two-forty-two, but that was in college. I think I came here at about two-thirty."

"You've gotta weigh more than that now," Bobby says as he locks the counterweight at 250 pounds and starts sliding the measuring weight across the arm. It finally balances out.

I stared at it, stunned. "That can't be right."

Bobby checks the scale to make sure it's accurate. He slides both weight markers to zero and we watch the little arm settle in the center of the bracket. It's dead-on. I've gained thirty-two pounds of muscle in ten weeks and I weigh a whopping 262 pounds.

I stare at my reflection in the mirror. Bobby tells me I look like a condo in cleats. I go home that night, dim the lights in the bathroom, and stand in front of the mirror, flexing. My chest is breathtakingly thick, my triceps are hanging flanks of beef, and my quads are like tree trunks. I've never been this big. It's frightening and extremely satisfying. But somehow I still don't feel big enough.

After a few moments I head over to the toilet, start to urinate, and notice that my urine is brownish. I turn the lights up and see that my urine isn't brown. It's red. I'm pissing blood.

A chill shoots up my spine as the word "Fuck" slips through my lips. I stare into the toilet for the longest time, hoping that maybe my eyes are playing tricks on me and it's something other than blood. But no matter how long I stare, or how many times I blink, the water remains a crimson hue. I was warned that Parabolin is toxic and not to stay on my cycle for more than eight weeks—but all drugs have warnings. Even an aspirin has a warning. But I know pissing blood means that something might be seriously wrong. I have to do something about it, but I don't trust the medical system in Italy after a bad experience at the dentist for a routine wisdom-tooth extraction. The dentist left me with a gaping big-enough-to-stick-my-entire-thumb-in-it hole in my gum. I asked him why there was such a big hole. He said, "Big tooth. Big hole."

I stand in the tiny bathroom for what seems like an eternity, trying to figure out what to do. Then I look back at the toilet, flush it, flip off the light, and go to bed, ending the struggle.

The phone wakes me at 4 a.m. I fumble for the receiver. "Hello?" I say in a voice heavy with sleep. There's a pause on the line. "Hello," I repeat harshly.

A mumbled, distant voice squeaks, "Dan, is that you?"

I recognize the voice immediately. It's Theresa, calling from the States. "Yeah?"

There's a long pause. Then in a hushed whisper she says, "You have a son."

I sit up in the dark and lean back against the wall, letting the receiver drop down, holding it with my shoulder. I have absolutely no idea what to say. When I left the States, there wasn't much of a conversation. I just said, "I'm going to Italy to play football. I'm leaving in two days." That was it. There was no long good-bye, no talk about the future. I simply got on the plane and left. Now, I've been in Italy for close to six months and I haven't talked to her once. I guess I kind of figured the situation would go away. A bad habit I fall into.

"Dan, are you there?"

"Uh . . . yeah. I'm here." I'm struggling to find something to say. I think about what is important right now. "Is he healthy?"

"Yes."

"Good, good." An awkward silence hangs thick in the air. "Okay . . . Thanks for letting me know," I say and hang up.

I sit in the darkness and whisper, *"I have a son."* I am struck by how oddly hard it is to say. I wait for a deluge of feelings to wash over me. Nothing. I say it again a little louder. "I have a son."

Still nothing. I don't feel a thing.

I start to panic because, regardless of my relationship with Theresa, this is supposed to *mean* something. I feel a wave of anger begin to rise. Why don't I *feel* anything? I turn and slam my fist into the concrete wall. *Damn it, feel something!* I punch the wall again and again. *Feel something, you fuck!* I keep pummeling away until the flesh on my knuckles splits open. I look down at my blood-covered knuckles and finally feel something. *Pain.* The sweet serenity of pain.

We win our next two games and are going to the play-offs. I'm still pissing blood and taking Parabolin, so I have no choice but to see a doctor. Fortunately, he's a teammate. He runs a bunch of tests on me and concludes that the Parabolin is affecting my kidneys. "Stop taking it immediately," he says.

"That's not an option," I say. "We're three wins away from the Super Bowl."

He stares at me long and hard. He knows I won't budge, so he gives me some medication and makes me promise to drink an extra gallon of water a day to help flush out my kidneys.

"I will," I say, "and I promise to get off the juice as soon as we win the Super Bowl."

I wake up in the beach town of Rimini and just know it's going to be a great day. It has to be. We won our first three play-off games and we're playing in the Italian Super Bowl this afternoon. I go to the field early to suck up some of the pregame glory. Moments like these don't last long, and I want to lap up every drop. It doesn't matter to me that this is the Italian Super Bowl in Rimini, not in America. These Italian guys are my teammates and play harder and care more than anyone else I've ever played with. They aren't playing for a scholarship or for money. They're playing for pride, and I'm proud to be playing with them.

On the first play of the game, I charge across the line and slam the running back in the backfield. The ball sputters out of his hands. Fumble. We recover it, but it comes at a cost. I exploded off the line with such ferocity, I reinjured my hamstring. I limp to the sideline. Bobby rushes toward me with an alarmed look on his face. I tell him it's the hamstring.

"There's no way we can beat these guys if you don't play," he says.

I look at the concerned faces surrounding me, my teammates for the last eight months. There is Mauro, who got me so drunk in the Chervania, I puked for two days. There is Alberto, who had sex with the transsexual. There is Francesco, who repeatedly had me over to dinner with his entire family, even though his wife couldn't cook worth shit. There is Bebo, who never took off his Ray-Bans and turned out to be a helluva coach. A brotherhood has formed. There's no way I'm not getting back on the field. They'll have to kill me first. I tell the trainer to wrap the hamstring as tightly as he can. He wraps layer upon layer of white athletic tape around my right thigh until it's as thick as a cast and I can barely lift it.

I hobble back on the field. For the next three hours, Bobby

Frasco, Dez, I, and our Italian cohorts fight like warrior gods in front of twenty thousand fans in the warm summer sun. When the clock ticks down and time expires, we reign victorious. We hop and holler and float on the clouds of victory as if we'd just won the NFL Super Bowl.

Later that night, while the rest of the team parties triumphantly at a local restaurant, I stay in my room and ice my hamstring. I know why the injury is back. And again, what is supposed to be my savior turns out to be the dagger.

I wonder, what makes it impossible for me to draw the line? How come I constantly edge over from use to abuse? Why do I need to burn to shine?

I suddenly remember I have a promise to keep. I struggle to my feet, unzip my suitcase, grab my stash of steroids, and lay them out on the bed. Vials of Parabolin and Deca gleam in evening light. Fool's gold. In one mighty sweep of the arm, I scoop them all up, toss them into the toilet, and flush. I'm done. Finished. Steroids are no longer a part of my life. I head out the door to join my partying teammates, feeling great. Better than I have in many years.

Frog teammates (left to right):
Bobby Frasco, myself, Bebo with his Ray-Bans, Marco, and Dez.

CHAPTER 7

Los Angeles Rams

I fumble for the phone in the dark. I hate being woken up by a ringing phone. "Hello?" I grumble into the receiver.

"Hi."

It's Theresa. Why is she calling me in the middle of the night again? Wait, wait, wait. It's not night, is it? I rub my eyes and notice the sun pouring in through the slits in the blinds. I have no idea where I am or why my head is throbbing.

"When did you get back?" she asks.

I slowly piece the puzzle together. That's right. I'm back in the States. I returned last night from Italy and went straight to the Red Onion to satisfy an insatiable craving for Mexican food and margaritas. More margaritas than food. Too many margaritas. My eyes glance at the clock. It's 11 a.m.

"Hey . . . look . . . I'm jet-lagged. I need to get some sleep. I'll call you later." I don't want to tell her how hungover I am or about the long-legged blonde from last night. No, she isn't in my bed this morning. She could've been, that would've been easy. But I don't think it would have been appropriate because I'm staying at my dad's house and my little brother and sister are around somewhere.

"When are you going to see your son?"

"I'll call you later." I hang up the phone. I haven't spoken to Theresa since the day she told me my son was born, and it is definitely not something I want to deal with right away. I cover my head with the pillow and drift off for some much-needed sleep. Drifting in and out of consciousness, I start to dream.

I'm alone in a grungy theater, planted in a red, crushed-velvet seat. The smell of damp cigarettes wafts into the air as a man dressed in a topcoat and hat appears center stage, his face painted white, with swaths of black under his eyes like something out of a Tim Burton nightmare. He speaks like a circus ringleader. "Good evening, ladies and gentlemen. For your viewing pleasure tonight I give you the one and the only, the incomparable Dan Clark!"

Suddenly, the theater is packed with rabid fans, dressed in tuxedos and evening gowns, roaring their approval. A single spotlight shines down from above, illuminating me in an effervescent glow as I revel in the thunderous applause. The ringmaster smiles, exposing his rotten, decaying teeth, and points to me. "Dan Clark. This is your life!"

The large curtains behind him whisk open to reveal a screen filled with flickering images of me as a four-year-old boy. I'm standing in the front yard of my childhood home, bright-eyed and full of optimism, dressed in a cheap, tan corduroy sport coat. My brother Randy appears next to me, flashing a killer grin.

I'm overwhelmed, crushed with emotion, as I sit in the audience watching my brother and me. I dab at my eye to brush back a tear. The audience gives a collective sigh of sympathy, with consoling pats on the shoulder. I nod my appreciation and mumble a handful of "Thank yous" like I've just won an award. A hand stays on my shoulder longer than it should. I shrug to get it off, then it

ping. The clock says it's 11:30 a.m. Shit, it's been only a half
r and she's already here.

"I wanted you to see him," she says, holding the bundle of life
toward me.

I get up and search for my pants. "What are you doing here? I
you I needed to get some rest." I'm stalling . . . doing whatever
n to keep from having to hold him.

"I know. But I thought you'd want to see him."

I look at her, then back at the ground, not sure what to do.

"Just *hold* him, Danny."

My mind rises up in revolt. *What happened to you not need-
anything from me! What the hell are you doing here?* Then I
my hands reaching for my son. The second I touch him, I feel
illion particles fracture inside me. It is overwhelming. It is big-
than I am. He seems impossibly heavy. My arms start to ache
the strength rapidly drains out of me.

"Here. Okay, I held him." I quickly hand him back to her.

I can lift five hundred pounds. But I can't lift the eight pounds
ounces that is my son. Deep inside . . . I know it's more than a
ld I'm lifting. It's a lifetime of responsibility that I'm not ready
. That, I cannot lift.

Theresa's entire body sags in the instant I give our son back to
r as if that moment crystallizes her worst fear. She will be raising
s child alone.

"Look, I gotta go." I slip my pants on and pull a T-shirt out of
 bag. "I have to talk to this agent about getting on a team." I zip
t the door. Who am I kidding? There's no agent. There's no
m.

n in full-blown steroid withdrawal. I count back, trying to figure
t how long I've been clean. It's been ten to twelve days and it feels
e I'm stretched out on a torture rack. Everything hurts. I'm weak
d constantly fatigued. There's a daily erosion of my mood—a

starts to clamp down on me and dig into my
and look down at the hand. The horrific-look
and burnt back to stubs with specks of bone a
for all to see. My eyes glisten with terror as I
scream. A hand shoots over it. I struggle to g
everywhere holding me in place, tearing at
they're trying to mutilate. My eyes bulge in ter
head and force me to look at the screen.

I'm on the screen, in the hospital in Vietna
as I can through dark, abandoned hallways. I
emergency-room doors and spill into a room w
an operating table covered in a white sheet. Wit
against my ribs, I approach the body, and I just
back the sheet, I'm going to be the one under it.
one who is dead. Finally, with fingers trembling,
the white sheet and stare at the pale, inert face.

It's not me under the sheet.

It's my brother.

The audience's faces break into hideous grins
of laughter. And I realize what the joke is. The j

The joke is . . . I'm the one who lived.

My eyes open. I'm back in my bedroom now,
blink hard, then dig my fingers into the sockets o
away and distance myself from the images of
That's when I notice someone else in the room.
wildly in my chest. I'm in the netherworld betw
consciousness. The person approaches me, silhou
streaming in through the shades. I'm about to scr
ize it's—

Theresa.

She crosses to the foot of the bed and says, "Th
I try to get my bearings. I have no idea how

chemically produced madness where my body is operating at a testosterone deficiency. I'm sleeping long hours and have little interest in doing anything. The mere act of getting up seems like a chore. And forget about sex. I meet a girl at the park and try to be intimate with her. Limp dick, nuts the size of raisins. I get dressed, tell her it isn't her, and slip out the door. I feel myself plunging into a black abyss as I go home and hop on the scale in the bathroom. I only weigh 250 now. I've lost twelve pounds in the ten days I've been in the States. I start to panic. I'm still huge and thick, but when I look in the mirror, I might as well be looking at an anorexic.

I can't take it anymore. I march into the bedroom, rifle through my drawer like a junkie, looking for the 'roids I'd stashed there before I went to Italy. I keep searching but I can't find anything. I'm manic until I remember that I put them in a shoebox up in the closet to keep them away from my younger brother and sisters.

I get the box and dump it over onto the bed. Like magnificent, priceless jewels, out falls Deca, Anavar, testosterone, syringes, alcohol swabs. I want to bury my face in them the way people do with piles of money in the movies. Instead, I snatch a bottle of Deca and a syringe, rush to bathroom, and pop off the little stopper. I stick the needle into the rubber topping and withdraw some of the liquid gold. I pull down my underwear, grab a fold of skin . . . until I catch my reflection in the mirror.

It stops me in my tracks. I'm desperate and disgusting. It makes me want to puke. I can't believe how much I need the drugs—how weak and dependent I've become. I tell myself, no drug is ever going to rule me. With that, I drop the syringe into the trash, go back into the bedroom, and gather up the rest of the drugs and stand over the waste bucket.

I feel my heart palpitate in my chest. I had no idea the enormity of the decision until now, as I'm staring it in the face. Throwing away the 'roids in Italy was easy. I knew I couldn't bring them back on the plane anyway. But to throw these away . . . feels like climbing a mountain. What if I need them for some reason? I don't have a supplier here anymore. My dad and Pete are no longer friends, and Dr. Kerr is in some kind of legal battle. Finally, I turn them upside down. The vials and pills clank around in the plastic trash can. This isn't good enough. I know I can't leave them here, too close, too much temptation. I take the little plastic trash can and dump it into the larger container outside. I don't totally relax until the next morning when I hear the trash truck come and haul off the container.

Two weeks later I get a call from Melvin Black, a buddy I played with in junior college who is now playing for the New England Patriots. He tells he can get me a tryout with the Pats. I'm on a plane the next day. The entire trip, I curse myself for throwing away my stash.

The night before the tryout, I go out to a club with Mel and All-Pro linebacker Andre Tippet. I'm absolutely amazed by the doors that open up when you're part of the entourage of NFL players. I'm not one yet, but being part of the group makes me feel important. At the club, we chat with Whitney Houston, Dionne Warwick, and a few other people I've only ever seen on TV.

The next day at the tryouts, I keep up with everyone in all the drills. I see the coaches talking and pointing in my direction. Then the forty-yard dash. Bang! The hamstring goes again. I'm screwed. No one wants an injured pony. For a thoroughbred, they'd place the bet and take a shot. On me, not a chance. But the little taste of the big time is addictive. I want more. There's nothing else I'd rather do in the world.

I come home, go to the local gym, and score some 'roids. My thinking is, *Steroids broke it. Steroids can fix it.* I know I just need to be smarter about it. Like a gambler in Vegas who just lost his house, I come back thinking I can beat it this time.

I walk into the bathroom holding the 2 cc vial marked DECA carefully in my hand. I stick my needle into the soft rubber stopper, flip the vial upside down, and draw out 1 cc of the liquid. I pull the needle out and tap the side of the syringe to bring the air bubbles to the top. I decide to stick it in my thigh. *A new baptismal. Maybe the results will be different.* I pinch a small fold of flesh between my thumb and first finger and slowly press the tip of the needle against my skin. Normally the injecting motion is quick, like throwing a dart. Not this time. I want to feel every bit of the syringe going into the muscle belly. I slowly keep pressing the needle against my skin until it punctures. I watch tranecelike as the needle disappears millimeter by millimeter into my thigh.

A small scream slips out from between my lips as searing pain shoots through my entire body like a blinding jolt of electricity. I grab on to my thigh with both hands and squeeze like hell, trying to pop the syringe out like the head on a pimple. Finally, I grab the syringe and tear it out. I hit a nerve.

Undeterred, I grab a fold of skin a quarter of an inch over and start the slow deliberate injection again. This time it's nice and clean. I slowly empty the syringe into my thigh, pull the needle out, pop an alcohol swab on the site, and massage the area. I tell myself it's just to help with the transition . . . that going cold turkey was a bad idea . . . that this is going to be a short "cutting cycle." Deca and Anavar, plus I'm going to diet. I know I have to drop some of the muscle and weight off because my frame can't handle it, which keeps perpetuating the hamstring injury. I also believe I need to stay in shape and be ready in case a team calls. Who am I kidding? Once again, there is no agent. There is no team.

That all changes on September 27, 1987, when the NFL players' association goes on strike and the team owners decide to continue with replacement players. It's an opportunity for another chance and I'm first in line.

Jim Kalafat shows up after the Rams strike for the same reasons as everyone else—getting that one-in-a-million chance to play in the NFL and, who knows, possibly catch the eye of a coach. Jim is an "all-everything" linebacker at Montana State University. He may not be the toughest kid ever to come out of Great Falls, Montana, but he's definitely somewhere near the top.

Whereas I *will* fight, Jim *loves* to fight.

There's no posturing or empty threats with Jim. He tells you to shut up, and if you don't, he'll crack you right in the jaw. At camp, we hit it off immediately and become best friends. We both have an insatiable passion not only for working out—all football players do that—but we also want to look good. We care about our body fat, the symmetrical lines of our torso, our biceps. Jim will later become Laser, of *American Gladiators*.

In the Los Angeles Rams locker room, steroids are openly discussed.

"Hey, what are you taking?"

"Anadrol."

"Me, too. Try adding some Wini. It'll cut you up."

"What about Equipoise?"

"Don't they give that shit to horses?"

"That's the only reason to take it."

If you look in the trash can, you can find syringe wrappers. It's quite common for players to walk into the bathroom stalls and inject themselves. The guy in the locker next to me keeps his stash out in the open. He doesn't care who sees. I openly discuss steroids, but never leave mine lying around. They're just too valuable.

I have no idea if this is how it's been in other NFL locker rooms. We're only scabs. But my assumption is the scene is not unusual. Sometimes I wonder if the NFL regulars got to where they are because they simply have better drugs. But I know that kind of thinking is the little green monster of envy, rearing its ugly head.

The players on the replacement team are a merry band of warriors from all different walks of life who still believe they've got game. I don't get to know any of them well, except for Jim. But I realize, yet again, I'm part of a rogue group of misfits, struggling to belong and find a place in the world. I say this with pride. I always knew I was a little different.

On the first night of training camp, Jim and I go out to the local Red Onion in Huntington Beach. As soon as we walk in, all eyes turn to us. We strut over to the bar and order a couple of drinks. Moments later, a girl saunters over and asks us if we're professional football players.

"Yeah." We nod, our chests puffed out with pride. "We play for the Rams," we say a little more quietly. I wait for her to ask if we're on strike, but apparently she doesn't know about the work stoppage.

She calls her friends over. "Hey, these guys are football players!" The next thing you know, we have five extremely attractive women fluttering around, sitting on our laps, drinking with us, and promising us things I can't repeat. I luxuriate in the attention, in being plucked out of the crowd, and being anointed special.

I look over at Jim and see something in his eyes. It rises as if out of nowhere, a brooding frown quickly turning into anger.

"Hey, is he looking at us?" Jim asks as he glares across the bar at some anonymous guy.

"Who?"

"That guy right over there." Jim's eyes bulge, he's ready to pounce.

I look across the bar. Who is he talking about? All I see is a couple of guys having a good time like everyone else.

"Right there." Jim points. "He's looking at us talking shit."

"No, he's—"

Before I can finish my sentence, Jim is out of his seat and on his way across the bar. The next thing I know, fists are flying, and we're in a brawl trying to beat the shit out of some guys because Jim thinks they were looking at us. This happens all the time.

During the strike I never worry about being called a scab or crossing the picket line. I don't care when the regular players stop the bus from coming into the practice facility and spit at the windows. I worked hard all of my life to play in the NFL and I believe in second chances. I believe that I belong here. My attitude is, I'm going to have some fun, play some ball, and show everyone what I can do. But as each week passes, the reality of getting cut becomes more apparent. We are like a platoon of doomed soldiers on our way to fight a battle we know we can't win. Maybe that's why Jim and I went from total strangers to the fastest of friends. The instability of the situation brought us together.

The strike lasts three games. A total of four weeks. The Rams like Jim and me and keep us around for another four or five games, then it's over. I'm distraught when I realize that my dreams are bigger than my abilities and I'm probably not a candidate for a pro football career. It's like the music stops but I'm still dancing. I know there has to be something else in life, if I can only figure out what it is.

CHAPTER 8

Busted

I carry a gun, a present from a girlfriend. I carry a gun because I have this deep, unshakable fear that I am never 100 percent safe. My girlfriend knew that I wanted one, that my dad always had one. My gun is a nickel-plated Colt Python, considered the Mercedes-Benz of .357 Magnums. Single-action, deadly accurate, with plenty of stopping-power. I take the gun with me wherever I go. I take it to Mexico.

I'm obsessed with body image, and my psychological dependence on steroids is rising to insane levels. Since I've returned from Italy, my drug sources in the States have dried up. Word on the street is that you can buy steroids right over the counter at the pharmacies in Mexico. But I have to be careful not to get popped coming back through customs. You're crossing a federal border, which means breaking federal laws that will elevate the trafficking and possession charges.

On a sunny Saturday, I drive down from Orange County past San Diego. The concrete jungle of poverty of Tijuana appears on the horizon. I've been warned not to buy in Tijuana. U.S. Customs agents have been known to lurk around and watch you buy steroids. Then they follow you to the border and pounce on you when you try to cross.

I stop in the beach town of Rosarito thirty miles from the U.S. border. *Farmacia* signs line the streets, seemingly at home with taco and pottery stands. I'm in no rush. It's Memorial Day weekend and I want to make a holiday out of it. But like a junkie in search of a fix, I pop into the first pharmacy on my side of the road to test the waters.

I tell the woman behind the counter in English that I want to buy steroids. She smiles and greets me like a long-lost friend, knowing instantly what I'm talking about. "You need a prescription," she says.

"What?" I ask, stunned.

"Pre-scrip-tion," she says slowly, like I don't understand her.

"I thought I didn't need one."

She shakes her head and tells me that I do. I storm out and go to two more pharmacies, only to get the same response. I need a prescription, but I quickly learn that I can get it at the pharmacy. They have a doctor in the back room behind a thin curtain. It's a total sham. I'm with the doctor only as long as it takes him to sign his name to the slip of paper and collect my $40.

I complain to the woman behind the counter. She tells me the prescription is for the Mexican police. The Federales' harassment of gringo tourists is legendary, but harmless if you cooperate. They'll pull you over and threaten to take you to the station, but they give you the option to handle the infraction, right there on the street, for a small cash payment. I've been to Mexico a few times to party and have never had a problem. I'm not afraid, and the truth is, I'm no gringo.

I buy Sustanon 250, the current steroid of choice. It's a veterinarian steroid made right in Mexico, a powerful compound made of four different types of testosterone. It's cheap, easy to get, and each dose comes preloaded in a syringe ready to inject. The problem with Sustanon is that it's hard to conceal. I buy fifty doses, meaning I have fifty full-size syringes, each wrapped individually in its own box.

I check into a beachside hotel to soak in some rays, down a few margaritas. But like a fiend, I can't wait to get to my room to shoot up. I fly up the stairs, charge into my room, drop my pants, and *bang*—slam the needle into my ass.

Doctors say it takes a few weeks to feel the effects of steroids. I disagree. I can taste the tinny oil the second I inject it, and I can feel it floating through my system immediately. It doesn't hit hard the way I read heroin does where your head drops back and you disappear into nirvana as the drug grabs you. It's more of a numbing softness that floats over me—an overall sense of well-being. The problems of life don't seem any smaller, but I feel bigger and more confident that I can handle them.

Being able to taste the 'roids immediately after injection is an ability that longtime users develop. When you first start taking steroids, you're in such a rushed state of anxiety, worried about your health, worried that you'll be discovered, that the taste slips by you. But then you become a connoisseur and can take the time to experiment and taste the different drugs.

I haven't been interested in sex for the past few weeks, but after the shot of Sustanon I have a ferocious hunger for sex. It leads me down to the hotel bar, filled with tourists and college girls. Jimmy Buffett's "Margaritaville" blares from a set of cheap speakers while drunken coeds and tourists dance in the sand as waitresses ply everyone with dollar shots of cheap tequila.

I do a lap, working my way through the crowded dance floor to let everyone know I'm here and to see if I can catch the eye of a girl lingering on me just a little longer than it should. Then I set up shop at the bar and wait for a girl to come to me. I'm not shy. I just can't stand rejection. I'm crushed by a simple no from a girl when

I ask her to dance. It's like she's saying no not only to the dance, she's rejecting me as a human being. I don't want to risk it, and usually and thankfully I don't have to. Most of the time a girl finds her way over to me inconspicuously, such as coming to the bar next to me and ordering a drink. Other times it's more blatant.

"Hi, my name is [you fill in the blank] and I [or my friend] want to meet you."

If a girl doesn't approach me or give that little window of opportunity to let me know she's interested, I go home alone. But I've never hidden my naked passion. I wear it on my sleeve like it's part of my uniform. Women know, they can sense, the tactile blast of kinetic sexual energy that's so palpable you can almost touch it. The surplus of testosterone surging through my body only adds to this. It goes below the surface and speaks to a woman's DNA.

But the woman is always in complete control. Women are the gatekeepers, the decision makers. They let a man know, they give the signal. Tonight, a girl lets me know that she isn't easy. She simply knows what she wants.

In the room, she's good. She can take it. I'm not talking about lovemaking. I'm talking about fucking. A good hard fucking. It's a world away from lovemaking. At this time in my life I don't know how to make love . . . or how to hold a woman . . . or to let a woman in . . . to really see her . . . and let her see me. The thought of this is beyond me.

I want porn sex. Not intimacy.

It's all about positions and duration, like an athletic event. It isn't sex. It's a performance. A lot of times I find girls who are game and good to go. Others simply can't keep up, and still others don't want to. It isn't what they signed up for. They're looking for love with me, which has them looking in all the wrong places.

I look back and wonder if I was trying to break their spirits, their will, and have them submit to me. Maybe it's the drug-fueled frenzy of testosterone and my DNA on overdrive, trying to keep the promise of our species and procreate. Or maybe it's the ideology of what it means to be a man in America. You aren't a man without constant, endless success. Manhood is a relentless test and I want and need to win here, too.

This was back then.

Back before I knew I was broken.

I get up early, way before dawn. I nudge her to see if she's good to go for another round. She holds up the proverbial white flag and says she's too sore. For some morbid reason I get supreme satisfaction out of this. It isn't "Hey, you're a good guy, I really like you." No that's too intimate, too scary. I don't know how to handle it. "I'm too sore" is something I can easily digest.

It's 5:15 a.m., still dark, when I get into the car and pull out onto the street with forty-nine Sustanon boxes taped under the backseat of my Jeep. I'm looking forward to getting home and back to the gym. It's the only thing in my life that makes sense. I like the purity of it: You get out what you put in. There's no cheating or lying, only a chemical assist. You train hard, you get results. Period.

Traffic is sparse in the darkness and a warm summer breeze billows up from the coast. My mind drifts to the girl from the night before, her scent still heavy on me. I think about what a life with her would be like—what a life with anyone could be like. Normally, I never think about a future with women. Their time with me is limited by how much fun they are. When the fun stops, we stop. Then I go out and find some new fun. It's simple and painless. A girlfriend once said, "You're easy to get, but hard to hold on to." I don't know if that's a compliment or an insult.

I push these thoughts out of my head, throw on Van Halen, and settle in for the long drive. David Lee Roth sings, *I live my life like there's no tomorrow. . . . Running with the devil.* That's when I notice red flashing lights in my rearview mirror. Not good. I'm not worried about the steroids. I have the prescription for them. I'm worried about my gun in the center console. These stops are customarily a shakedown, a chance for the local cops to make a few extra bucks. They pull you over, make up some obscure offense that you've committed, then give you the option of either going to jail or paying the fine on the spot.

I pull over on the highway. Two Federales roll up to my left. Through the dirty windshield in the dim light, I can see one of them motioning me to get off at the exit. I look up ahead. It's a barren road that leads into deserted darkness. There's no fucking way I'm getting off a well-lit highway before six in the morning and driving down some back road that leads to who the hell knows where.

The Federale comes up right next to me and shines his flashlight directly into my face, blinding me. He says in broken English, "You. Drive over there."

Every cell in my body tells me not to do it. I shake my head no. There's a moment of confusion. They exchange words between themselves in short, angry bursts. I get the sense this isn't the way they want it to go. They don't expect some American not to comply. Moments later a craggy-faced Federale appears in the light. He's pissed. "You drive down there, now!" he barks in broken English.

I start to panic, not sure what to do. I know I've got the gun in the car and I don't want to cause too much of a commotion too soon or it could lead to serious trouble. Slowly, I put the car in gear and roll down the off-ramp into the darkness until the road levels out. My mind flashes. *A barren road. A killing field.*

Seconds later, Craggy Face screams, "Get out of the car!"

"What did I do wrong?"

"Get out of the car!"

His face is corrugated with scars. He is big for a Mexican. He's reaching for my door.

"Okay, okay, I'm getting out. I don't want any problems."

His partner is there, too. Younger, but still big enough to be a problem.

All I can think about is my gun in the center console as I exit the car. "Look, I'm not sure what I did wrong, but whatever it is, I'm happy to take care of it," I say as I reach for my wallet. Craggy Face tells me to get up against the car. An alarm goes off in my mind. *Oh, shit! They don't want money. This is bad. Very bad.* I hope they're just trying to intimidate me to get a bigger payday.

I put my hands against the car, turn my back toward them, but keep a sharp eye on both of them. If a blow is coming, I want to see it. This way I'll at least have a chance. Craggy shines his flash light in the car . . . across the seats . . . the floor . . . the glove box.

I'm aware they might be intimidated by my size. I try to diffuse the situation again. "Amigo. I'm sorry if I did something wrong. Tell me how to fix it. Tell me what you want me to—"

The younger cop jabs me in the ribs with his nightstick.

I wince and grunt audibly. He thinks it's funny and jabs me in the ribs again.

This time I don't make a noise. I just grit my teeth. I'm scared shitless.

The younger Federale steps forward. He's inches from my ear. I can smell the booze on his breath. I don't like him this close.

Craggy Face barks something at him in Spanish. He takes a step back and is now behind me where I can't see him. A voice flashes in my head.

THEY ARE GOING TO KILL YOU.

The message is so clear it makes me look into the darkness to see if some unknown person is out there.

THEY ARE GOING TO KILL YOU, the voice blares again.

I don't trust it and try to shut it out. If I listen to it, I'll have to fight.

THEY ARE GOING TO KILL YOU, the voice screams in my head, shattering any sense of doubt.

As my eyes dart, looking for a place to run, I see the nightstick out of the corner of my eye flashing toward my head. Acting on nothing but instinct, I shoot my arm up and deflect the blow. I smash his face with my elbow, turn, and hit him as hard as I can.

He crumbles to the ground as Craggy Face reaches for his billy club. I explode into him and drive him back into the car door with all 235 pounds of me. We hit it with a thud, slam to the ground, and roll. I end up on top of him, one hand on his wrist with the club, holding it plastered to the ground. The other is around his neck, choking the life out of him. He's screaming at me in Spanish full of rage.

I want to smash his face in. I want to kill him. I grab a handful of Craggy Face's hair and smash the back of his head into the concrete until he's just a groaning mess. I spring to my feet unsure of what to do next. My eyes rapidly survey the area. The two cops on the ground. Their police car's engine is still running. My Jeep. The sun rapidly rising over the mountainside. Wait—there's something about their car. My eyes dart back to it. It doesn't have the police emblem on it. I cross over to their vehicle and look inside. No police radio. No shotgun rack. No glass or bars separating the front from the back.

Only the stupid magnet siren on top of the car. These guys aren't cops. They're criminals.

I don't know if I'm more relieved or scared. I take their keys, jump into my Jeep, and speed off, running for my life. I keep my eyes peeled to the rearview mirror. I don't relax until I get to the border and am sitting in my car in front of a U.S. customs officer. But the next thing I know, he orders me onward to secondary inspection.

I pull under a covered area with concrete barriers blocking the way in front of me. Cars in various stages of disassembly are slotted along, with customs agents searching through them. A bald-headed bull of an agent approaches me and asks, "What're you bringing back from Mexico?"

"Nothing," I say, trying to fight the nerves twanging up the back of my neck.

He considers me for a moment, then says, "Would you step out of the car, please."

I don't move. I have a decision to make. Do I tell him about the gun?

His face takes on a new level of seriousness. "Sir, would you please step out of the car."

I decide it's best to come clean. At least this way he'll know I'm being up-front with him, and maybe after the disclosure, just maybe, he'll be satisfied and let me go. I slowly put my hands up on the steering wheel, so they're both in plain sight and not a threat.

"Before I get out of the car, I want to let you know there is a loaded firearm in the center console."

The next thing I know, I'm on my stomach, eating asphalt, with guns pointed at the back of my head and people screaming at me, "Don't move! Don't fucking move! Stay down!"

I'm handcuffed and brought to a holding room. Moments later, my forty-nine boxes of Sustanon are dumped onto a table. Bald-Headed is reading me the riot act, firing off my list of infractions: drug trafficking, smuggling, possession, unlawful transportation of firearms, crossing an international border . . . the list goes on and on. He tells me how fucked I am, how much trouble I'm in, how I'm looking at ten years of hard time. I say nothing. I have no excuse.

Moments later, the commanding officer enters. A silver-haired man close to fifty, he reminds me of my father. With him, there is no screaming. There are no threats. He asks me questions. Lots of questions. And he listens.

I tell him the truth. I have the gun in the car, which is registered to me, because I've been target shooting in Mexico and forgot to properly store it because I left early in the morning to beat the traffic at the crossing. I tell him I'm just out of college and I bought the steroids because I'm trying to get on an NFL team and can't get them in the States anymore.

He asks if the steroids are all for me. I nod that they are, and I tell him I'm not a criminal. I just want to play football and need to take them to compete.

He asks me how much they cost. I tell him $119.

He focuses intently on me for a deep moment and tells me this is a serious offense and I could be in a lot of trouble.

I nod that I know and I say, "I'm sorry."

He exits and leaves me to suffer through the thoughts of my diminished future.

Minutes later, I hear Bald-Headed and the commanding officer arguing outside my door. Bald-Headed keeps shouting, "Zero tolerance! Zero tolerance! What happened to zero tolerance!"

There is a hard silence, then I hear Bald-Headed yell, "This is bullshit!" His voice grinds to silence and I hear the sound of shuffling feet. Seconds later, my door opens. Silver-Haired enters and tells me to stand and turn around. He uncuffs me.

I blink at him in a confused moment. "You're letting me go?"

He nods that he is and tells me they're confiscating the drugs and my gun and I'll have to pay a fine of $119, the amount of the drugs I was trying to bring across the border. He also tells me I'll have to go to court in San Diego for unlawful transportation of a firearm.

"Thank you," I say, crushed by his mercy.

He looks at me for a long beat, then quietly says, "I have a son . . ."

I stare at him, blinking furiously as the words that are a key to my freedom reverberate through my brain. The same four words I find so difficult to say.

I get home that evening and call Theresa.

I tell her, "I want to see my son."

I pick him up the next day, and at six months old he spends his first night with me. A few months later, I make a court appearance in San Diego on the unlawful-transportation-of-a-weapon charge. I get three years' probation. I'm a lucky son of a bitch.

CHAPTER 9

I'm on TV!

"Hey, do you want to be on TV?"

"Get the hell outta here!" I say.

"Seriously," says Floyd Raglin. "I can get you both on a TV show."

Jim Kalafat and I are talking to Floyd on a summer day at the South Coast Plaza Mall in Santa Ana, California. We've known Floyd from the football world, and we saw him last night on the HBO television show *First & Ten,* a sitcom about a fictional football team called the California Bulls, starring none other than O. J. Simpson as T. D. Parker as the general manager of the team, a decade before Simpson's arrest and trial for the murder of his ex-wife Nicole, and her friend Ron Goldman.

Floyd tells us he is in charge of recruiting football players for *First & Ten.* We were former pro players—we were shoo-ins. The pay for nonhitting days is a hundred bucks. For days on the field, we get $150 base pay, plus bumps for special stunt plays and big hits.

Let me get this straight. I'm going to be on TV and they're paying *me*?

Jim and I drive up to L.A. that day to check it out with Floyd. We have lunch at Chin Chin's on Sunset Boulevard, smack in the middle of Hollywood. This is the heart of "cool"—big city and bright lights. Floyd knows the two long-legged models at the table next to us and calls them over to our table to join us for lunch. It's a surreal moment, the epitome of a Hollywood lunch, with people hiding under hats and sunglasses, sipping on iced teas. I feel out of place in my pink Izod shirt, plaid shorts, and Top-Siders. People are different in L.A. They're cool. Dark. Mysterious. Everyone seems famous and Floyd is on TV. He's in with the "in" crowd.

Stars in our eyes, Jim and I pack our bags and move to Hollywood immediately to work on *First & Ten*. I'm confident that in no time we'll be hanging out in Beverly Hills with Sly, Arnold, and Eddie. What I don't know is that Floyd is an *extra*, and that we are going to be extras, too. I've never heard the term and have no idea what it means. But I learn quickly that in "Hollywood speak," being an extra means *We have the right to treat you like shit*.

The first day on the set of *First & Ten*, we shoot scenes on the practice field at El Camino College in full football gear. The stars of the show are talking to the director. I have a question for him, so I make my way over. A pasty-faced assistant director stops me in my tracks and tells me I can't talk to the director. If I have a question, I have to ask him. Then, if he can't answer it, he'll ask the director. I tell him this makes absolutely no sense. The director is right there, five feet away. If I have a question for him, I'm going to ask him.

"Well, you can't," the assistant says with a scowl.

"Why not?"

"Because I said so." He walks toward me like he's going to do something. I'm stunned that this little guy is even *thinking* about getting in my face. Pointing his chubby finger at me he says, "Now, you, go away."

Anger shoots through my veins. I'm gonna smash his head in.

I step toward him and loom over him so he can feel my spit on his cheeks. "If you ever put your finger in my face again, I'm going to snap the fucker off and shove it so far up your ass, you won't shit for a year."

He turns sheet white and his face starts to twitch. "Floyd!" he hollers, his voice cracking with fear. Floyd quickly hustles over with a few other people and stands between us. I stare through them at the guy, still intent on ripping his head off. Floyd pulls me away while the others comfort the coward. I explain the story to Floyd fully, expecting him to back me up.

Floyd blinks at me. "He's right, Dan. You can't talk to the director. The director only deals with the people with speaking parts."

"That's the stupidest thing I've ever heard."

Floyd looks at me squarely. "It's different here. *It's Hollywood.*"

"It's Hollywood" is a hard pill for me to swallow. I have naively assumed that if you work in Hollywood, you're on the "team" and are friends with the stars. That's the way it is in football. It doesn't matter if you're first, second, or third string. You sleep in the same hotels, shower and dress in the same locker rooms—you're part of the team, part of the family. In Hollywood, there are the stars, and then there's everyone else.

Furthermore, with a speaking part, your salary goes up to $400 dollars a day from $100. But a first-year guy can't get a speaking part. Players have to pay their dues and toil as extras for a season before they are considered for a speaking part. I watch in disgust as everyone clamors around the director like circus seals, yelping for a treat—hoping to get a line.

Here I am pretending to be a professional football player on a fictional team because I can't make it into the NFL. Just great. Just fucking great. The players on the *First & Ten* team are mostly a hodgepodge of high school athletes and actors who are athletic. The skill level isn't horrible, but everything is choreographed. For each play, we know exactly where the ball is going. The toughest part is trying to sell it and make it seem real. There is no testing of your skills against an opponent. There is no sneaking through the line and leveling the quarterback with a bone-crushing hit. *There is no glory.*

Another thing that I find absolutely ludicrous is the filming of scenes off the football field. For the locker room scenes or scenes with the team at the bar, we have to mime words and can't actually speak when they're shooting. That way we won't step on the actors' lines. So, first I'm pretending to play football, then I'm pretending to talk. It's a new pecking order and I'm at the bottom. Well, not the very bottom. At least I'm a "featured extra," not a "feed you the brown bag for lunch, sit out in the cold, herd you like cattle" extra. My football history distinguishes me a little bit, but no one really cares that my team won the Italian Super Bowl, I played with the Rams, and I can bench close to five hundred pounds. I suddenly feel like I'm living in a world that wasn't built for me.

But there are good times, too, like when one of my hero linebackers, Lawrence Taylor, the giant of all Giants, joins the show and plays Tombstone Packer. On the field, LT is an explosive force who wreaks havoc on NFL offenses every Sunday. But off the field, the fury that makes LT a future Hall of Fame player put him on a runaway blitz to self-destruction. I experience this firsthand when we walk off the white lines of the fictional football field into the alluring "white lines" of the Hollywood party scene. LT parties like a rock star. Cocaine is the only thing he can't tackle with ease.

O. J. Simpson is another hero of mine. (Well, at least he was back then.) The most vivid memory I have of O.J., before the Ford Bronco Chase, the bloody glove, the "If it doesn't fit, you must acquit," is the revolving door of his trailer. O.J. always has a line of beauties waiting to get into his trailer. Someone tries to pass off that they're hoping to get a piece of memorabilia. Memorabilia? They got some.

Working with O.J. and LT is an indelible experience. Fat with meaning. Two of my heroes. Two flawed men.

Like my father.

Like me.

I take a quick inventory of my life. I'm twenty-three years old, my football career is a wash, I'm a little different from the next guy. I have a few hundred dollars in the bank, an apartment, and a CJ-7 Jeep. I don't have much, but I *do* have an overwhelming belief in myself. A belief that I can be the best at something. Not that I'm special. Rather, I feel the opposite is true, so I spend my time knocking down doors, looking for a way to shine.

I feel bulletproof. Or maybe I don't know how to feel. I do know how to fight for something I want, and if I don't get it, I know how to correct the course of action and then keep trying until I succeed. And I know how it feels to fail. That's why I push so hard for success. I know how it feels not to matter. That's why I abuse my body with steroids. I know how it feels to think I don't deserve to live. That's why I'm willing to die trying . . . to matter . . . to be someone . . . to be something . . . to deserve to live.

Steroids or no steroids, I have a work ethic, and my immediate goal is to get a speaking part. I send out letters and pics to agents, trying to land one. One hundred sent. Zero callbacks. I have to think of a better way. On paper, I'm just a guy. In person, I'm not so easy to ignore—which is why I'm knocking on Joe Kolkowitz's door. Joe is a crotchety guy, born in a foul mood and bald at twenty-five. If you call central casting and say you need a cantankerous Jewish agent, Joe is what you get.

"Yeah, what can I help you with?" he says as he opens the door.

"I saw your name in this book for acting agents. It says you specialize in athletes."

"Yeah, so?" He acts like my very existence is annoying him.

"I'm an ex-professional football player and I'm working on *First & Ten*."

His eyes show a glimmer of interest. "Really? Do you have a speaking part?"

Damn, there's that speaking-part bullshit again. "Uh . . . no."

He's instantly bored, like I just wasted a year's worth of his time. "Leave your picture and résumé in the box."

I look at the box. It's stacked full of pictures and résumés, as are his desk and his shelves—literally hundreds upon hundreds of pictures are everywhere in his office. I'm astonished by how many people are trying to make it in Hollywood. And this guy is a smaller agent. If I put my picture there with the others, it'll fall into a bottomless pit of obscurity.

"Look, just give me a shot at something. I won't let you down," I plead.

"I'm really busy. You're going to have to leave." He starts shooing me out the door.

I shove my foot in the door. "I'm not leaving until you find me something."

I watch as his mind flutters through a bevy of thoughts. He's considering his options. He can call security and have me removed or toss me a bone. He throws up his arms and says, "What the hell. There's an audition for football players at Twentieth Century–Fox for a movie with Mark Harmon called *Worth Winning*. Swing by there, pick up your *sides*, and I'll get you an appointment for next week." He scribbles the address on a piece of paper and hands it to me.

"Thanks! Thank you," I say gratefully. "I won't let you down. You'll see!" I start to leave but I turn back, confused about something. "Sorry to bother you, but what am I supposed to pick up at Fox?"

He looks at me like I'm suddenly the bane of his existence again and repeats, "Your sides."

"Oh! Okay. Yeah, yeah, yeah. Got it," I say, acting like I know exactly what he's talking about. I thank him profusely again and march off, with no idea what "sides" are.

I get in my car and drive over to the casting office. I beeline toward a Drew Barrymore–type blonde behind the desk. "Hi, I'm Dan Clark, I'm here to . . ." I hesitate. "I'm here to, I think . . . to pick up or give you my *si . . . sizes.*"

As the words came out of my mouth, they feel right. That's what Joe must've said, they want my "sizes."

"Have you already been cast?"

"I don't think so," I say, suddenly overcome by a wave of insecurity.

She gazes at me for a quick beat, then says, "Give me a second. I'll be right back." She exits, then returns a few moments later. "I just talked to the casting director. She has you down for an appointment for next Thursday at three p.m., but said she doesn't need your sizes unless you've been cast."

"Oh, okay." I shrug, confused as hell. "Thanks."

I head to the door with a nagging feeling that something is not right. Then it hits me. This must be a joke they play on all the rookies. We do it in football and they must do it in this business, too. You send the big dumb guy to the studio and make him look like an ass by asking for some stupid thing he doesn't need. I half expect a *Candid Camera* crew to pop out or balloons and streamers to fall from the ceiling. Joe's probably keeled over on his desk laughing right now, and they're going to burst into laughter as soon as I walk out of here. Ha, ha, funny. *Okay, you got me,* I think as I hit the door.

"Dan!" the Barrymore blonde calls out from behind the desk.

I turn to look at her. *Here it comes. Go ahead, make fun of me.*

"Do you want to get your sides before you go?"

My face cracks in confusion.

"There, on the table over there." She points to a box. I study her for a beat, not sure if this is part of the joke. Then I slowly walk over to the table with a stack of script pages. On top of the page it says, "Sides for Football Players." I start to laugh because I suddenly realize that "sides" are scenes pulled from the script to read for the audition.

"Grab the one that says Rick. You'll be reading for that part."

I swoop them up, stoked and relieved. I'm actually going to get to say something or, at the very least, audition to say something. I just know in my heart that this is my big break. I can feel it with every fiber of my body.

I study my lines day and night. I'm told by an actor friend to try the lines on real people to see if I'm believable. I walk into 7-Eleven and bark at the Indian guy behind the counter, "I don't know what she sees in a guy like you, but if you touch her, I'll rip your head off!"

He pales and shrinks back. "Hey, buddy, I don't want any problems. Leave or I'll call the police."

I think, *Wow! I must be good. I just scared the shit outta him.*

On the day of the big audition, I'm nervous as hell. More nervous than I was playing in front of seventy thousand people. Sitting in the casting office, I'm in a cold sweat and can barely breathe. *Relax, relax,* I keep telling myself, but my heart won't stop hammering in my chest.

When my turn finally arrives, I enter the tiny room. The casting director, Joanne Zaluski, introduces herself and tells me she'll be reading with me. She gives me the option of either standing up or sitting down. I sit, then stand. Sit, then stand again, then sit again. I tell her I'm almost ready. That I need a moment. Suddenly I decide standing is better. I rise to my feet and decide that *pacing* would be even better. I start to pace back and forth across the room like a caged animal. I'm really going to let her have it. I'm going to let her feel my fury. I even *growl* at her. "Grrrrr." I can't tell if she's afraid or amused. She reads the first line. I blurt out my line—and that's last thing I remember.

The next thing I know, she's thanking me for coming and escorting me out of the room. I blacked out in there and I can't remember anything that happened after that first line. I walk out of the office in a daze, feeling like I've had my bell rung on the football field. As I drive home in my Jeep, I replay the scene over in my head. I'm pretty sure I said my lines. Well, at least I think I did. Shit, I'm not sure. The only thing I'm absolutely sure of is *my first audition was a complete disaster*!

I stomp into my apartment, furious with myself. How could I blow such an opportunity? This was my chance to hurtle out of the primordial soup of Hollywood into the world of speaking parts and I blacked out. I march up to my bathroom, fling open a drawer, rip out a syringe, and load up a fat shot of Primobolan. As I drop my pants and bury the syringe into my thigh, the phone rings.

My machine picks up on the first ring and I hear "Dan, it's Joe Kolkowitz from Sports Casting. The casting office called and they want to know your availability."

My heart leaps. Available? Am I available? Are they kidding? Pants around my ankles, syringe still buried in my thigh, I scamper across the room.

"They need to know right away. Dan, are you there?"

I shuffle my feet in little rapid bursts, ignoring the sudden pain in my thigh from the dangling syringe, and scuttle toward the phone.

"Damn it, I guess you're not—"

No, no, no. Don't hang up! I leap across the bed, grab the phone.

"Joe, it's me, Dan!"

"Hey, they really liked you. You got the—"

Suddenly I screamed bloody murder. *"Ahhhh!"* I look down and realize I've landed on the syringe and bent the needle in my thigh.

"Dan? Are you okay?"

"Yee—ees," I grunt through gritted teeth.

"Well, you got the part. You work next week on the seventeenth. Are you available?"

"Th-th-th-at's great. I'm s-s-s-oo happy," I hiss, trying to use my happy voice, but it comes out more like an I'm-being-raped-in-prison squeal.

Joe starts talking about agency contracts, SAG papers, work dates, wardrobes. The pain is mind-numbing. I can't focus on a word he's saying. "Joe, can you please hold on?" I barely manage to get the words out. I lower the phone. I rip out the syringe and scream again.

That's how I get my first part in Hollywood.

I can't wait for the seventeenth to arrive. I'm like a kid waiting for Christmas. Every morning, I mark off the days on the calendar waiting for the big one. I practice my lines every chance I get. This is going to be a huge moment for me. I'll finally be able to actually talk to the director. I think about the different ways the lines can be said . . . where I can put the accent. Each place I stress it, it gives the entire sentence new meaning. It's maddening.

The day finally arrives. I drive to the Fox lot. My name is on the list (niiice!) and the guard ushers me to my own parking spot. Niiice. My own trailer. Niiice. I go and get my makeup done. Niiice. Mr. Clark, can I get you something to drink? Niiice. It's good to be the king.

I pull out my sides and practice my lines as I walk back to my trailer. This is it. I have finally arrived. I'm finally going to get to talk to the director. As I enter my trailer, I notice FOOTBALL PLAYER NUMBER TWO written in bold letters above the door. Errrr! The sound of brakes slamming. I look at it again. FOOTBALL PLAYER NUMBER TWO. That's odd. I'm playing Rick.

I walk to the trailers on either side of me. FOOTBALL PLAYER NUMBER ONE. FOOTBALL PLAYER NUMBER THREE. I venture farther and find FOOTBALL PLAYER NUMBER FOUR. I march back to my trailer and there it is, staring back at me like an epithet: FOOTBALL PLAYER NUMBER TWO. I find the assistant director and tell him there must be some kind of mistake. I was hired to play Rick, but my dressing room says FOOTBALL PLAYER NUMBER TWO over it. He looks up my name and tells me I'm wrong. Someone else is playing

Rick and I am football player number two. I ask him if he's sure. He tells me he is.

I'm thunderstruck and squeak out, "Do I at least have any lines?"

He shakes his head no. I tell him I want to talk to the director and clear this up. He tells me I can't. "The director only talks to people with speaking parts."

Back to square one.

Me with Lawrence Taylor.

CHAPTER 10

Gladiator

The sitcom *Mr. Belvedere* needs someone to carry furniture in a scene—I'm their guy. The soap opera *Santa Barbara* wants a guy to wear a patch over one eye—there I am. Budweiser needs a buff guy on the beach for a commercial—sign me up. Need a guy to wrestle another guy in a Speedo? Look no further—I'm your man. (Yeah, I actually did it.) I go from knocking down quarterbacks to knocking down small parts in Hollywood.

The big problem is that the "guy" isn't making a living. *Mr. Belvedere* pays me $86. Budweiser doles out $100. *Santa Barbara*, not much more. Speedo wrestling pays $250. Rent $450. Car $220. Steroids $200. Child support $300. Then throw in insurance, gas, utilities, phone. You do the math. The Hollywood dream is running on fumes. I'm down to my last couple of hundred dollars and I have to borrow money from a girlfriend to help pay for last month's rent. Forget about this month's rent.

I think about dealing steroids, but it just isn't in my blood after the fiasco in Mexico. Theresa invites me to come stay with her in Orange County. She has my life all planned out: live with her, get student loans, go to law school, then start to work for her sugar daddy's law firm. I'm haunted by the idea of disappearing into obscurity, of being a regular guy.

I don't know what it is, but I know there is something out there for me.

I look into trying out for an NFL team, but can't get a tryout. The arena league has started; I go and try out there. But I can't hook up with a team. I'm like a soldier who can't make the transition to peacetime. I miss the violence of the game. I miss and need a place to work out my juiced-up energy. I need a place to call home.

I go down to Orange County to see my son. I sit with Theresa in her house. She's going on and on about what I should do—about what kind of job I should get. Just saying the word *job* makes me want to smash my head into a wall. A *job* means I've failed.

I want to live a life.

I want to rise to the heavens.

I want to matter.

I don't want to get a damn job.

Suddenly I can't breathe. I have a sense of the world orbiting around me while I'm standing still. I have to get out of Theresa's house. I hop in my car and breathe. I look out across the horizon and see a thunderstorm rolling in. My face is devoid of expression. Just a silhouette against the angry sky. I'm astonished how quickly I went from a life where everything seemed obtainable to one in which it's difficult to grasp on to anything with certainty.

Most of all, I don't trust Theresa. I see her as a barracuda in a skirt. I'll never forget the day she came to my dad's house, before I moved to L.A., with her sugar-daddy boss. At the time I wasn't sure what role he played. Years later, I'm sure she gave him a little sniff to get the car, the house, the bowling ball with her name on it. They ambushed me in the driveway, serving me with papers asking me to give up parental rights to my son.

She never filed the papers, but for years she held them over my head like a guillotine. I didn't feel wanted as a kid and I'm horrified my son will feel not wanted. It isn't that I don't want my son. It's that I don't want a life with his mother—and I'm not ready for a son at twenty-three.

I drive aimlessly around the city, then pull up to my mother's house and sit there in my parked car for hours. I think about how hard my mom works at her factory. I think about her driving across the country in the little Pinto to see me. I think about how tough her life has been since she came over from Japan. I think about how she never had a chance to pursue a dream.

I think about my brother. Dead at twelve. He never had a chance to dream.

The thought rattles in my brain and gets trapped there, like a ball bouncing repeatedly off a wall. Suddenly I'm furious. I'm shaking and trembling and trying to choke it back and control myself. I know I need to calm down, I just don't know how. I start the car and race off down the street. I can't control the adrenaline dump . . . the rage.

Never had a chance to dream.

I'm lost in a blind fury. I start punching the roof of my Jeep. I'm so mad, I can't see straight—I can't drive. I think I'm gonna puke, so I pull over. I'm out of the car and running through the darkness for all I'm worth. Down the city streets . . . past parked cars . . . dilapidated buildings . . . and the graffiti-covered walls of my diseased life.

Never had a chance.

I'm trying to run through the rage. To get to the other side. Breathe. Run. Faster. Harder. I burst out of the mouth of an alley into the morning sun spilling over the horizon. I'm in front of my old high school. I drop to my knees. Gasping. Sucking in air. The anger still surging. Calm down. Breathe. I squeeze my eyes shut. I tense every muscle in my body.

I'm shaking. Squeeze harder. Blackness now.

Then the images come roaring back like a fantastic dream. I'm back where I want to be. In the locker room . . . at the games . . . in the school corridors . . . with my teammates . . . the victories and defeats . . . the triumphs and the shared pain. I'm at the place where I found my identity. Where I dared to dream. A place where life was simple and pure. A calmness slides over me. I know what I need to do.

I borrow money to pay the rent and head back to Los Angeles with the understanding that I have one more month to try to get a decent job in the business. If I don't, I'll head back to Orange County, to possibly finish school or . . . get a job.

The month quickly evaporates into a week. Seven more days until I walk away from the world of dreams into mundane obscurity. I call my dad and tell him I might be moving back to Orange County. My confession is met with dead silence. I know how much of his emotion and energy and life are wrapped up in my career and seem to hinge on it. Maybe he thinks if my star burns bright enough, it will spill over onto him and illuminate the dark places in his life. Torching the failures.

I go for a workout. I keep training because I'm still holding on to the dream. But as I leave the gym, I tell Angel, the owner of Hollywood Gold's Gym, to cancel my membership on Monday. I'm not coming back. I'm moving back to the OC. I head out of the gym feeling like a complete failure. I pull into the local 7-Eleven and grab a copy of *Backstage West,* a Hollywood-industry weekly magazine, as a souvenir to remind me of my time in Los Angeles.

That's when I read about the audition:

LOOKING FOR ATHLETES WHO ARE GOOD IN
FRONT OF THE CAMERA FOR A NEW GAME SHOW.

It might as well have said:

"DAN CLARK, WE'RE LOOKING FOR YOU!"

The audition is at Barrington Park in Brentwood that same afternoon. I rush over there as fast as I can. When I step onto the field for the tryout, there is no bellowing chant of my name. There is no burst of applause. No cheerleaders. No hope of being picked up by an NFL team. San Jose State, the Rams, the Italian Super Bowl that rocked my world, seem like a millennium before. In ten months I have become an afterthought. I feel like I've been forgotten and dumped on the waiver wire of life.

There is no shame or self-pity. There is the hope and the belief that I can be the best at something. In front of me, strewn across the practice field, are a hundred other hopefuls, dressed in workout gear, lingering like cattle waiting to be herded through auditions. As I eye my competition, a select few look good or stand out, but I keep thinking about audition notice: "Looking for athletes who are good in front of the camera." I've seen O.J. act, as well as LT, Roger Craig, and a few other NFL actor hopefuls. I know they can crush me on the field, but there's no way they can touch me in front of the camera. I know I have a bit of chutzpah they don't.

I trust my combination of speed and aggression can take me through every drill. As I line up for the first one, I suddenly realize how much I miss the contact of football. I miss hitting someone and getting hit by someone. I blaze through the push-ups, sit-ups, tire obstacle courses, and other similar exercises and keep thinking, *Just give me someone to hit,* because I know I can do it with such viciousness, it will separate me from the poseurs. I don't want to bully anyone. Rather, within the confines of what is legal and fair, I want to hit someone with everything I have, because in those brief moments everything makes sense.

I think about how I have always stayed in shape because I held on to the dream of finding a place to shine. About how I've continued to work out when people were telling me there was no point. Because I knew I had to be ready if I wanted to win. I knew that to

win I couldn't just do what everyone else was doing. To win, I had to do what no one else was willing to do.

Today there is no winning or hitting. After the workout is over, the producer pulls a few people over and asks them to stay for an on-camera portion of the audition. I am among them. They hand the dozen or so of us three character profiles and tell us to choose one. Once we choose, they're going to ask us questions, and we have to respond in character. I zip over the list.

Gemini: A huge mountain of a man with a split personality. He is a gentle giant one moment, a killer the next. Well, that could be anybody on the 'roids.

Malibu: The cool, laid-back surfer. Two hundred twenty pounds of twisted steel and sex appeal.

Nitro: Loud, explosive, cocky, bad-to-the-bone character that never lets anyone forget he's in the room.

Something about the Nitro character speaks to me. Something about the rage and the anger that I feel comfortable with . . . something about the desire to be seen.

They flick the camera on me and fire a salvo of questions.

What's your favorite movie?

Terminator.

What do you eat?

Raw meat.

What are your thoughts about competing?

Destruction.

I can look back now and chuckle, but back then it was all very serious. It was more than a job. It was survival.

The final audition is held at a soundstage at Universal Studios where they bring in a bunch of students from Cal State Northridge to "test" games for a new game show. The students think it's going to be something along the lines of *Jeopardy* or *Wheel of Fortune.* Then they see me and the other finalists for *American Gladiators.*

I am completely ripped, totally juiced, and I face off with a student in a mock football drill where I am the tackler/defender and he is the running back—a game that will later be called Breakthrough and Conquer. All the student has to do is get by me and score a touchdown. By the way, did I mention we're standing on concrete when this college boy tries to make $75 for his education, attempting to run the football past me?

Pumped to the max with steroids and righteous rage, I slam the ball carrier to the concrete, knocking him out cold. A hush fills the soundstage, a medic rushes to the kid, and a producer rushes over to me. I'm absolutely sure I'm to be fired and quickly escorted off the lot when the producer whispers in my ear, "You've got the job."

My very first question is "How much does it pay?" They tell me it's around $7,500. I quickly calculate the numbers in my head and figure the money will help extend the lease on my "Hollywood life" for about six months. My second question is "*What's* the job?" There are no costumes yet, no sets, only a character breakdown and chalk lines on the concrete floor of a Universal Studios soundstage.

"It's going to be an athletic competition where normal people go up against larger-than-life athletes in events to win money and prizes," replies the producer.

"Cool," I respond. But the truth is, I don't care what it is. All I care about is that I'm getting paid and I'm going to be on television. I look at another producer and say, "There are two things I need to know. One—this is going to happen, right?"

He nods, guaranteeing me that it will.

"Two. I'm going to be able to *hit* people, right?"

This makes him smile from ear to ear. It's exactly what he wants to hear.

Nitro is born. I am unleashed.

I immediately take the stance: *Nitro isn't where attitude happens. Nitro is where it lives.*

CHAPTER 11

Becoming a Star!

"Unbelievable. Just unbelievable!"

That's what I think as I walk onto the cavernous *American Gladiators* stage on the Universal lot for the first time. I stop at the mouth of the arena, a sheet of blackness in front of me. I inhale deeply to savor this moment. As I close my eyes and imagine a packed house with ten thousand people cheering rabidly, overcome with fervor and Nitro-mania, I hear a horn explode and rise above the pandemonium. Then I hear a voice:

"Hey, buddy! Get outta the way!"

I turn to see an irate driver and a forklift stacked with crates behind me.

"I'm a Gladiator," I say.

He looks at me blankly.

I soon discover that I'm on the wrong stage.

That's how seven illustrious years of *American Gladiators* begins for me. It doesn't get much better as I enter our stage. This first year we are a work in progress—human lab rats put to the test to build a better mousetrap. As imperfect, basic, and barbaric as

this first season is with its cold concrete floors—walk-the-plank jousting platform and the human-cannonball suicide podium—it is beautiful. We are just a little show . . . not yet in the media glare. There is a freedom. A lawlessness. We all care . . . but we aren't a hit. So we grope along and find our way as the show progresses. This is when we are still innocent.

Today, most people know about *American Gladiators*, but here's something you probably don't know. Raye Hollitt (Zap) is the only Gladiator who didn't have to audition. Raye, five feet two inches, blonde with mounds of muscle, gets the part of Zap because she's coming off a big movie, *Skin Deep*, with the late John Ritter. Raye is one of the first women who are extremely buff and still feminine. Hell, she was prom queen at her high school in Pennsylvania.

Does Raye Hollitt take steroids? I don't know. I've never given her a shot, I never saw her take a shot, and she never told me she took a shot or swallowed a 'roid. Do I think she takes steroids? Don't know. Don't care. That's her business, and if she wants to tell her story, I'll stand in line and buy the book like everyone else. I'm not here to "pimp my 'roid." I'm here to tell the truth and the facts, as I know them.

Here's what I do know. Raye is blonde, buxom, athletic, and strikes like lightning—gets in fast and causes a lot of damage. That's what she does to competitors. When I first meet her, I'm in awe. She is easily the most muscular woman I've ever met, she's been in a big movie, and people stop her on the street. Her body stands in such juxtaposition to her face. She's as big and as strong as any man her size, but her face is kind and gentle with an indefatigable smile that brightens any room.

Over the years, I have discovered, the more muscular the girl, the more they like to be treated with tenderness in the bedroom. At first they might want to dominate a man, because that's often a man's fantasy with muscular women: "Wow, I'd like to be sandwiched between those thighs." But when it comes down to it, most really muscular women want to be treated like ladies, very femi-

nine, which oddly enough is the very thing they build their bodies to combat.

Gemini, aka Big Mike, one of the male Gladiators, is a man among boys. I look up to and respect him. In the first years he is the glue that held us Gladiators together. A calming force. He is a fierce but always fair competitor with a heart bigger than his biceps. Big Mike is the patriarch of *American Gladiators* and one of my best friends. He has an easiness about him and I gravitate toward him. He's like a big-brother figure, the rock and the foundation and the captain of the team. I never want to be the captain of the team. I've never been the captain of any team. To me, being a captain is a managerial position that implies a sense of leadership. I'd rather float around the edges with a sense of lawlessness and recklessness. It's my need to be unleashed and my chemical madness, my induced "aggressive" style of play.

Meet Lace. The minute I see Marisa, I'm stunned by how startlingly attractive and sexy she is. She's been in the biz for a while. She's tasted the glory by marrying a film star, Michael Paré of *Eddie and the Cruisers* and *Streets of Fire* fame, so she knows the deal. She's about the same age as the rest of us, but has the weariness of someone who has seen too much. You can see it in her eyes, behind her smile. You can see it in her eyes twenty years later when *TMZ* reports she's been arrested for possession of narcotics.

Then there's Malibu. Deron McBee, a future viral sensation on YouTube, is built like an Adonis. Perfectly cast in the part of the laid-back surfer, he has a beautiful mane of blond hair that gives Farrah a run for her money. He has massive delts, thundering arms, ripped abs, and skinny legs.

Skinny legs? Big problem.

Athletes need a strong base, and Deron is like one of those houses hanging over the cliff in the Hollywood Hills, supported by two scrawny little beams. Sure, they look great, might even make the cover of architectural digest, gleaming in the summer light. But would I want to live there during a big earthquake? Not a chance.

American Gladiators is an earthquake of a show, and Deron's stilts can't support him. He comes tumbling down after the first thirteen episodes. D has no experience in playing contact sports. He was a pro-level racquetball player, but he didn't play a lick of football, never wrestled, nor done anything that has a physical element to it. Getting smacked in the face takes some getting used to, and Deron just doesn't have time to adjust.

Now that you know the Gladiators, understand that we follow the golden rule:

You can't make the fight come to you. It has to be in you.

The first thirteen episodes are the hardest (I'd go on to do 131 more). There is virtually no budget and we test the games as we perform them. I can't believe the stupid shit we tried. We used an executioner in a mask to decide the outcome of close calls by standing over the Gladiator and the contender and giving a thumbs-up or thumbs-down call. That's how it was the first year. No instant replay. No Diamond Vision screen. Just a ref dressed in an executioner's mask.

During the first season there is virtually no audience. The producers make a deal with Universal to give the studio free publicity in exchange for making the Gladiators part of their world-famous studio-tour tram ride. Families who come to the entertainment capital of the world for thrills and excitement hop on the tram and get the shit scared out of them by King Kong and the shark from *Jaws*. They get their spirits lifted by driving past little E.T. murmuring, "Phone home," with his little heart-light blinking. Then they get the ultimate up-close experience of being in the audience on a working set while an actual television show is being filmed—the *American Gladiators*!

There are a couple of huge problems with this idea. First, *Gladiators* hasn't aired yet and no one knows who the hell we are. Tourists discover a world of buff, oiled bodies, glimmering in red, white, and blue spandex. Second, it's our first year and there are so many technical problems, the episodes take an ungodly amount of

time to shoot. Even on a good day, shooting a television show is an ordeal. We have to strike the set in between every event . . . camera malfunctions . . . electrical malfunctions . . . and we don't know what the hell we're doing.

Soon we have crying kids and angry parents demanding to leave. When the pages tell them they can't, the audience revolts and leaves anyway. They aren't going to get stuck spending the day watching some stupid show they've never heard of when they've shelled out $49.50 to get into the park and have the ultimate Hollywood experience.

It's disheartening to us. I suddenly feel stupid, all oiled up and dressed in skintight spandex, when there is a mass exodus of the audience. A lot of us ask ourselves what the hell we've gotten ourselves into. Production stalls. Without people in the audience, we can't shoot. I keep thinking, *Don't cancel the show in the middle of the production. I need the money.*

A set designer comes up with the idea of putting plywood up around the arena and painting faces on it to make it look like there's an audience behind the few people who are actually in the audience. That, and they dim the lights. The producers agree it's worth a shot, so Big Mike and I watch them paint the faces on the plywood. We look at each and shrug: "Oh, boy, this show is never going to make it."

Production continues, and we don't get any more of an audience, but we hit our stride and we have great contenders such as Billy Wirth (the actor), Eldon Kidd, Brian Hudson, Bridget Venturi. Something about *American Gladiators* is pure, an intangible, making it different from anything else on television. But after the first thirteen episodes wrap, I don't think any of us see it coming back. I figure I have just enough money to live for six months, so I better find another job fast. We all shake hands, hug, and talk about how much fun it was, and we hope we get to work together again. We don't know that we've forever changed the landscape of television.

———

The show's been over for a week, and during that time I realize, for the first time, that I'm happy with what I'm doing. I'd been forever locked up in my limitations, unable to tap the talent and wonderfulness inside me. I knew it was there but I hadn't had a chance to let it out. To let it shine.

The producers send Malibu and me to San Francisco to do publicity for the show before it airs. They put us up at an excellent hotel and tell us to order anything we want from room service. For breakfast Malibu and I each order a twelve-egg-white omelet, a steak, grapefruit, and a carafe of orange juice. The bill for each of our breakfasts is over $100. After that, the producers quickly opt to give us per diem pay instead.

I have my first inkling that the show might be something special when I pull out of my apartment on Arch Drive in Studio City, make a right on Ventura, then run smack into a giant billboard of myself and the rest of the Gladiators. Staring up at it, mesmerized, I almost drive off the road into a fire hydrant. I hop out of the car and gawk at the billboard, riveted. I feel high, like none of this is real, like if I blink, it will all be over and gone. I stop a man walking past me.

"Excuse me. Do you see that billboard?"

"Uh . . . yeah." He looks at me like I'm a freak.

"That's me!" I beam. "That's me on the billboard!"

"Uh, yeah. Whatever," he mutters, and walks off.

I forget it's L.A. Everybody is on a billboard. Or think they will be.

The show airs, the numbers are good, and we quickly get the pickup for the second half of the first season. Now I am getting recognized, and it's a real rush. I savor the experience when someone looks at me, his face lit up in recognition, and says, "Wow, aren't you Nitro?" It's about a thousand kilowatts stronger than "Aren't

you a football player?" It feels like someone is saying, "I love you. You're beautiful. You're special. You're someone."

Before we began to shoot the second half of season one, I walk my buddy Jim Kalafat into the producer's office. Jim and I are rooming together, and I think he'll make a great addition to the show. "This guy is a stud," I tell them. "A fierce competitor. If we're adding a Gladiator, he'd be the guy." They agree and Laser is born. Another guy they add is David Nelson, Titan. And let me tell you, he is a brick shithouse of a guy. Not quite six feet tall, he weighs nearly three hundred pounds and he's strong as hell. He says he used to be a running back in college. I look at his thick frame and wonder what in the hell he's eating.

As the next batch of episodes approaches, I'm obsessed with what type of steroid cycle would be best for a Gladiator. I want size and strength, but I also want to be ripped and lean like Hercules. I want to look like a bodybuilder, but hit like a Mack truck. I opt for Anavar with Winstrol V, a veterinary drug, used for cutting. The problem with Winstrol is that it's water-based, it keeps getting stuck in the needle, and it hurts like shit when I inject it. I keep using it, thinking it's a small price to pay for glory.

On a warm Los Angeles Saturday afternoon a Rolls-Royce pulls into the parking lot of Universal Studios during the second season and parks in front of our soundstage. Out steps a bearded, sculpted mountain of a man who literally blocks out the sun. It's Lyle Alzado, the most feared man in football. I now know *Gladiators* is a hit because in Hollywood people travel to power, and Lyle Alzado has come to us.

He isn't frightening in person. Although a giant of a man, he is soft-spoken and self-deprecating. He is here visiting Lace, Marisa. I can't remember if they're dating or just good friends. It doesn't matter. This is 1989 and Lyle Alzado is a huge star. He's fought Muhammad Ali and announced a huge, much publicized comeback

with the Oakland Raiders. He's opened a restaurant in the heart of Hollywood. And he's just *denied* taking steroids on a prime-time interview with Maria Shriver, wife of Arnold Schwarzenegger, on NBC. When asked about steroids, he replied, "Just because an athlete is built well, and he works hard and he trains hard, it doesn't necessarily mean he has to be on steroids. I'm clean. I've always been clean, and I'm gonna stay clean."

Just as I thought Floyd had made it in Hollywood when I initially saw him on *First & Ten* as an extra, I think Alzado has it made and is living on easy street. I don't know he's struggling at a crossroads in his life. Sure, the bit parts in movies still keep him busy, but he isn't happy. Not that this job would necessarily make him happy. In Hollywood, you're always a day away from being a has-been, and one movie or part from being a star again.

We go to dinner that night at Lyle's restaurant, "Alzado's," and the guy can't be a more gracious host. He treats us like we're the celebrities. We sit at his table, order whatever we want off the menu, and Lyle covers it all. When I get him alone for a minute, I ask him about steroids. In direct contrast to his television interview with Maria Shriver, Lyle is candid about his use as we compare cycles. Usually the bigger the guy, the more he's ingesting. But my mouth drops open in awe when Lyle tells me what he's taking . . . Equipoise, bolasterone, Winstrol, Anavar, test cypionate, and a couple of others I've barely even heard of.

The restaurant is packed and I think Lyle must've misunderstood my question. I don't want to know all the different steroids he's taken throughout life. I just want to know which of these drugs he's *currently* taking.

"No, Lyle. I want to know which of these drugs are you cycling right now? I mean, you look fucking great."

"All of them."

I'm stunned.

"I'm taking all of them," he repeats slowly, intoxicated by my surprise.

"At the same time?"

"Yep," he says like a proud papa holding his newborn.

I still can't believe it. "Really?"

Lyle puts one of his meaty paws on my shoulder. "Dan, it's either go big or go home."

Words of advice. Words that will prove to be a death sentence.

Lyle slings his thick arm over my shoulder and pulls me in tight. We walk back toward the table and join the party. It's hard for me to focus for the rest of the night, even though there are women, mounds of blow, and a lot of good times to be had. All I can think about is the massive cycle Alzado is taking. I watch him throughout the evening, going from table to table, telling his war stories and entertaining. Lyle reminds me of my father back in the early days in Vietnam at Wally's restaurant. They are the same bundle of charisma and machismo, the reason their namesake restaurants are successful. They are both my heroes at the time.

Lyle is the toast of Hollywood. He's healthy, charismatic, and vibrant—the life of the party. He is everything I want to be. He's my idol. So much so that I go home and make the most outrageous steroid cocktail I can conjure. I clean out the entire medicine cabinet and dump all the bottles of injectables on the counter.

There's cypionate, propionate, testosterone suspension, Primobolan, Deca, and Equipoise. Some bottles are full and others barely have a cc left in them. I check the expiration dates as I fill the syringe with different drugs. First is the cypionate, 2 cc. Then 1 cc of Equipoise, followed by popping the ampoule of Primobolan and sucking 1 cc into the syringe. Now I put in 1 cc of Deca, and 1 cc of suspension. I still have a little room in the 6 cc syringe so I grab the propionate. It has already expired. What the fuck, I don't care. I pull back the plunger, fill the syringe to the max, and hold it up to the gleaming light. My last thought before I empty the syringe into my ass is, I'm going to be just like Lyle. As I depress the plunger, I'm suddenly haunted by the words of F. Scott Fitzgerald: "Show me a hero and I'll write you a tragedy."

That night, I wake up in a cold sweat, my heart palpitating, my head on fire. I rush over to the toilet and vomit flies everywhere. I lie on the floor. My system can't handle the overload. My chest is clamping down on me. I pick up the phone to dial 911. *Breathe. Just breathe. Call them now. You're going to die.* I slam the phone down, rush into the bathroom, and rip open the medicine cabinet. I need to find a way to slow down. I can't call 911, it'll make the headlines: "Gladiator OD's on Steroids." I wonder if it's possible. My mind gets stuck there. Not wanting to face the truth. The pain. I'm not overdosing. I'm having a—my heart is hammering so fast and clenching so tight. I feel a sudden spasm shudder through my chest, pulling my shoulder blades back. My whole body is splitting with pain. I drop to my knees. I pick up the phone again and call my girlfriend Sabrina. I tell her I think—I'm having a—heart attack.

When she arrives, I'm crumpled in the corner naked and shaking with pain. She begs me to go to the doctor.

"I can't! I fucking can't!"

"Why?" she screams.

I grab my chest as a new wave of pain smashes into me.

Sabrina starts to cry. "Dan, please go to the doctor!"

"No! Goddamn it! No!"

The pain is overwhelming. Searing. I curl into the fetal position and squeeze every muscle in my body as hard as I can.

Sabrina starts to cry harder, touching my forehead. "You're burning up. What happened?" Her eyes search and she sees the remnants of my steroid cocktail strewn across the counter—enough to open a pharmacy. "You're a fucking idiot!" she screams. "Damn you! I'm calling the hospital." Sabrina heads for the phone.

I shoot a hand out and grab her. "You can't! Please . . . don't! Please. I just need something to slow my heart down."

Sabrina stares at me, deciding. Then she rifles through the bathroom drawers and finds a bottle of the muscle relaxer Soma. She cracks the lid and dumps a couple into my trembling hand.

"More," I say.

Sabrina keeps pouring until I have a fistful. I swallow them back in one mighty swig, then grab the base of the toilet to fight off a new wave of pain. I vomit, spewing everything across the back of the toilet, then slump back down on the bathroom floor. "More," I plead.

Sabrina dumps the rest of the bottle in my hand. I chug them back and do everything I can not to vomit again. I need the Soma in my body to slow down my heart or I could die. Sabrina stays by my side the entire night. Comforting me. Holding me. She knows I've been taking steroids. She found a syringe in my bathroom a few months ago. Back then I told her not to worry about it, everyone I know takes them. She swallowed the explanation because she'd never seen any of the side effects. Until now.

This is the last time I ever see Sabrina.

She doesn't want to be part of my crazy, fucked-up world.

Sabrina and I in happier times.

CHAPTER 12

'Roid Rage

It starts like any other fight. The harsh exchange of words, chests puffed out, and egos the size of Texas. The other guy stands tall at six feet one inch with 225 pounds of hard-forged muscle. He isn't just big. He's so ripped, his neck looks like a Scud missile.

My heart bangs against my rib cage, my mouth goes dirt dry, and my breath comes in short, wispy gasps. The physical sensations before I get into any fight are always the same.

"Screw you!" he screams at me.

I turn sideways to a forty-five-degree angle, dip my chin behind my slightly raised left shoulder, and look up at him. I'm lining him up. Still the nerves are there as I desperately struggle to keep my courage and to form my words so he can't hear the tremor in my voice.

"Back off, man," I say.

It's a scorching March night in Palm Springs. Rice rockets, with thong-clad girls on the back, race up and down the street. The boulevard is a mixture of sex and drugs. I'm here to celebrate the time-honored tradition of spring break and to bask in the glory of

my newfound celebrity since *Gladiators* has just finished a successful second season. People are recognizing me on the street, I have
money in the bank, a new car I just paid cash for—and here I am,
pulled over to the side of the road, about "to throw" with this
enormous guy. How in the hell did I get into this mess?

The truth is that I don't really want to fight. I want to be picking up one of the bikini-clad girls, I want to be drinking a Patrón
margarita on the rocks, I want to be anywhere except where I
am—about to have a fight.

My ego won't let me just walk away. He's picked the wrong
guy on the wrong night. I can tell by the smug look on his face that
he feels the same way. After all, he called me out, so I had no choice
but to pull my Jeep to the side of the road and meet the challenge.

*You can't back down, I tell myself. You can't let them think
you're weak. You do it once, and every punk will challenge you,
thinking he can take you. Even worse, you'll know. You can live
with fear, but you can't live with being a coward. Once, when you
were fifteen, you walked out of the room. Never let it happen
again.*

I study him closely. He's a big mother. I wonder if I can beat
him. I know this guy has been in a lot of fights and he's pumped out
of his mind on 'roids. Just like me. Frankly, he scares me, but I'm
okay with that. Fear is good. Fear keeps me on my toes—keeps the
adrenaline and the rage teetering on the red line.

*If he breeches my safe zone, my early-warning system, I'll fire
on him.*

All fighters like to keep people a certain distance away from
them. Someone crosses it, once—you might give him a chance.
Twice—he's going down.

He suddenly closes the distance between us, reaches up to grab
my shirt.

Bang!

I unleash a hard right, backed by 230 pounds of rage, right into
the side of his face. An involuntary "Ohhhhh" escapes from the

open mouths of the onlookers. I back off, waiting for him to drop. But not this guy. He's tough as nails. There's no sign of immediate pain on his face, only an ashen look from the blood deserting it.

He fires back at me. Fast and furious. I have no time to think. I answer with my fists. We're lost in a barrage of punches and kicks as more cars pull over and the crowd swells to a mob. We hit the ground hard and the crowd hears the sickening crack of bone on pavement. We roll, punching and gouging at one another, looking more like savage beasts tearing at each other than human beings.

I'm lost in the rage, the blind fury. It's as if someone has flipped a switch and opened the floodgates. The world slips away and I'm at one with my opponent as I hammer and punch him with every-thing I've got. There's a "maddening peace" in being beyond thought, lost in consensual violence. It's pure and satisfying. I feel acutely alive, primal, and at the same time afraid. With each punch given or received, the rage seeps out of me in explosive spurts. A fight is what I need, what I'm aching for.

I'm on top of him now. I have the advantage and I continue to rain blows down on him, quenching that ache inside me every time I connect. He's writhing on the ground now, covering his face. I stop for a quick inventory of the mess I'm hopefully mak-ing of his face. My mistake. Too much rage drains out of my body and I give him an opening. He unleashes a bombardment of crush-ing blows, stunning me. Then he yanks me down into a headlock and starts choking me. The guy is as strong as a silverback gorilla. I struggle, but I'm starting to lose consciousness, my world giving over to black. He starts to punish me with crunching blows to the rib cage.

Even though I feel his fist crunching into my ribs, I don't regis-ter the pain. My rage is back and it blocks the pain. Pure instinct kicks in as I start to fight for my life, punching viciously at any open spot my fists can find. I connect again and again, hurting him badly. He becomes desperate, which makes him even more danger-ous, because he'll do anything to survive. He flings out a beefy arm, collars my neck, and rips me back down into a vise grip of a head-lock. Our faces smash against each other.

This is when I hear it—a deep guttural growl, then the snapping and chomping of teeth. It sounds like a rabid pit bull buzzing toward my ear. Instinctively I jerk back when I feel his teeth sinking into the flesh of my cheek. I try to pull away, but I can't—he's biting me, gnawing on the side of my face. A stinging surge of pain jolts through me. It quickly dissipates when I become overwhelmed with the thought *This guy is biting me! I can't believe he's fucking biting me!*

I slam a forearm into his throat with such force it causes him to cry out. I pull away, scramble to my feet, touch my cheek, and stare at my fingers. They're red with blood. I'm stunned. I feel a new wave of rage and I want to go ballistic on the guy, but it wouldn't be right. He's lying on the ground, not trying to attack. It's kind of an unspoken truce between fighters that we both have had enough. I extend a hand to help him up.

As he reaches for it, I keep thinking, *He bit me in the face!* I can't let it go. It keeps rattling in my brain. He has crossed some kind of moral line. You don't bite someone in the face during a fight! Just as he grabs my hand—

Bang!

I fire on him again. My knuckles slam into his face and he crumples to the ground. It's a cheap shot, the lowest of lows, but I figure he has it coming.

People jump in and restrain us. That's okay. I don't want to fight anymore. I've had enough.

The crowd buzzes around us. I stare at my opponent, who is bleeding, thinking, *What the hell just happened?* I'm so sick about it I can feel the bile rise in the back of my throat. My opponent looks up at me and says, "Fuck it, Dan."

How'd he know my name?

He is my best friend. Jim, Laser of the Gladiators.

How did it start?

We were driving in my Jeep down the strip toward the Red Onion, got into a meaningless argument, pulled over, and got into a fight.

Standing there in the sweltering heat, I feel pathetic. I feel I'm at the mercy of my rage. I am its victim. My mind is peppered with thoughts of my life before steroids when I wasn't so quick-tempered, when I'd never let my fists sling that freely. But I realize that on the juice I am a different kind of person. After discovering steroids, my rage ebbed and flowed with ease. I led with my temper and followed with my fists. If I won a fight, my wounds were badges of honor and I was proud to display them. But not now, not tonight. Deep down, I am becoming a person I despise.

"We cool?" Jim asks, climbing to his feet.

I nod. "We're cool."

We pull each other in for a hug and a couple of slaps on the back. The crowd cheers. Jim and I hop back into the car like nothing happened, and we race toward the Red Onion to go drinking.

As we make our way from the parking lot to the Red Onion entrance, I catch our reflection in a glass window. The sight of us washes over me in a wave of grief. We look like hell. Our clothes are ripped, my left eye is battered black-and-blue, and my cheek is spewing blood. Jim has a lump on his forehead the size of a tennis ball and scrapes cover his elbows and knees.

No matter how we look, we still want to party. We are in Palm Springs, juiced up and drunk with youth, power, and invincibility.

Jim looks at me and at the entrance to the Red Onion and says, "They're never going to let us in."

I chew on this for a quick second. Then I look back at him and say with all the confidence in the world, "Yes, they will. We're Gladiators."

Smiles spread across our faces as we walk toward the entrance, our arms slung over each other's shoulders.

I am right. They let us in and we drink for free. That's how it is these days.

CHAPTER 13

Excuse Me!
I Think I Just Kissed a Guy

"You're beautiful."

I can tell by the searching look in her eyes she doesn't believe me.

"Really . . . I think you're fucking beautiful."

She still doesn't believe me. I take both of her hands in mine and look directly into her eyes. She turns away.

"It's hard for you to take, isn't it?"

She can't speak and simply nods.

I brush a wisp of hair out of her eyes. They're full of tears.

Angie is beautiful. She has cinnamon-brown, soulful eyes that I could get lost in, a butt that a guy would eat a mile of shit just to get close to. But for some reason, she doesn't see it. Angie used to be a competitive bodybuilder, but those days are long behind her. She now works as a receptionist at a law firm, but I've seen pictures of her when she was competing. She was a monster. Thick, muscular, and solid, with sixteen-inch arms. Not my type at all. But since

123

then, she's shed her man-suit, and all that training left her with a fabulous figure.

I first met her at an appearance for *Gladiators*. Angie isn't the kind of girl to parade around in front of you clamoring for attention. She hangs in the background and waits for you to notice her. I'm scanning the faces of the crowd when our eyes meet. She looks away bashfully and I go back to signing pictures. An hour later, I check the crowd and she's still there, smiling and lying low. When the appearance is over, she hangs around without seeming like she's waiting for me.

I approach her and we start to talk. She puts out a warning: "I'm not the kind of girl who just jumps into bed with a guy."

I smile at her. "I wouldn't have it any other way."

I also know this is a lie. The girls who say this are usually the first ones to hop in bed with a man. I'm not saying they normally hop into bed with a lot of men. I just know this statement is usually a disclaimer for the sins they're about to commit with me.

But I'm wrong about Angie. It takes us a few weeks before we finally find our way to the bedroom. We sit on the edge of my bed kissing, about to take it to the next level, when she starts to cry. Crying before sex is unusual, but I guess it's better than crying during sex, and definitely a helluva lot better than crying after sex. That can only mean trouble: "I didn't want to . . . I'm married . . . I love you . . . I'm pregnant . . . You're done already?"

"What's the matter?" I ask.

"You know I used to take steroids," she says, dabbing at her tears.

"Yeah . . . I saw some pictures of you when you were competing, so I kind of figured. But don't worry about it."

"You've taken them, right?"

I hesitate for a second. Thrown. Women don't normally ask. If they do, I usually deny it. It's just easier. There aren't so many questions to answer. But because Angie has been so forthright, I feel comfortable telling her the truth:

"Yeah. I have."

"For how long?"

"Do you really want to know?"

She nods that she does.

"Okay . . . let me think about it for a second. I started on my eighteenth birthday . . . then there was five years of college . . . the year in Italy . . . the Rams . . . and I've been up here in L.A. for three years . . . so that's . . . uh . . . *ten years*."

Her face stretches in surprise. "Really?"

"Yeah . . . I think." The truth is that steroids have become such an integral part of my life, I stopped counting years ago. But when she gets me to consider, I have no choice but to confront the reality. Just the thought of taking the 'roids for ten years makes me weary. I think about the people and the places drugs have taken me. From Mexico to Italy . . . from puking into the toilet and pissing blood . . . to fighting in the streets . . . to getting arrested. I'm suddenly exhausted and I feel dirty.

"Any side effects?" she asks.

"Do you really want to have this conversation?"

"Yes."

"Why?"

"I'm curious . . ."

I lie back on the bed, put my hands underneath my head, and stare up at the ceiling. This isn't my idea of foreplay. But I'm game. It's interesting because I've never had a conversation with a woman about the side effects of 'roids. I'm always trying to hide the side effects . . . not plop them out in the open for her to see. I think about it for a moment longer, then in a quiet voice speckled with shame I say, "A lot of times, I just want to beat the fuck out of someone."

The words hang thick in the air. I shift on the bed, uncomfortable, but the truth is, it feels good just to say it. To voice what I feel the majority of my waking life. "It's really weird. Sometimes I find myself in a minor argument, and the next thing you know, I've got my hands around someone's neck trying to strangle him. It's like the rage is bigger than I am, and in the snap of a finger it goes from zero to full-fledged fucking fury. I can feel it coming . . . but there's nothing I can do about it. And then I'm beating the shit outta someone."

I look at her for a reaction, or perhaps a condemnation. But there isn't one. She simply rolls toward me, puts a leg comfortably over mine, and props her head up in her hands, listening attentively.

"Other times I feel like I just wanna die. I've got so much shit and energy flowing through my body and I can't get it out. I'm not suicidal or anything, but it's the only way I know how to explain it. It's fucking frightening."

She looks at me fascinated, like I am her very own science project.

"And there's other times I want to cry . . . I wanna scream and put my head through the fucking wall. It's just that . . . that . . ." I can't find the right words.

"Go on. I want to hear."

"It's just that . . . I feel . . . I feel like I'm always *chasing* something or *running* from it . . . and it's maddening because I can't find that place in the middle where it's still . . . and everything slows down . . . so I can just . . . I can just . . . *be*."

I exhale deeply. It feels good to try to put words to the torrent that has been going on inside me. And it's true. Some of the time, I feel bulletproof, like no one can touch me, and other times I feel fucking awful . . . like a failure.

There is no middle ground. Just moments of relief.

Angie starts to kiss me hungrily. This momentary glimpse into my soul ignites her. It does the same thing to me. I want to be in this woman. Not just fuck her. But be deep in her in a place I can't touch . . . only feel . . . where we can fall off the cliff and be lost in the abyss of sex, sweat, and passion.

I slip her top off. Her body is stunning. Tan, lean, with full natural breasts. But I don't want to spend too much time there too soon. I move back up so we are face-to-face and grab a handful of hair and softly pull. Her head falls back and she lets out a soft moan. My hand quickly finds the zipper of her jean skirt. As I flick open the snap-over button and start to unzip it, she stops me.

"No . . . no. Not yet. I want to talk."

I'm done talking. That window has closed. I'm overcome with desire for her. For that moment. For that place.

She sticks a firm hand into my side, pushing me away. "I'm serious. I want to talk."

I grunt in frustration, roll away from her, and sit up in bed, feet dangling over the side, doing everything I can to control myself.

"Don't go away from me, please," she pleads.

"Look, I just started a cycle of test and my hormones are through the roof, so this start/stop stuff is killing me. And you're starting to weird me out. You're just a little too interested in steroids. What's your deal? Are you a reporter or something?"

She crawls behind me, gently drapes her arm over my shoulder, and hugs and kisses me. "Come on . . . just a little more. I want to know more about the side effects." She's like a strung-out addict needing a fix. I can't understand it.

"You're driving me fucking crazy. You know that?"

"It's just that . . . I had some side effects from them and I wanted to know what yours are," she mutters.

"Oh, kind of like sharing war stories?" I grin at her, a mischievous look on my face. "Okay, I'll tell you anything you want to know, only if I get to fuck you after."

Hurt splashes across her face. Immediately I know it was the wrong thing to say. I try to see her eyes, but she won't look at me. I'm confused. This is all new to me. Why is she so interested in steroids?

"Okay. . . . You really want to know?" I say, trying to see her eyes again. She throws a cutting glance at me. I decide to talk freely. "Let me see . . . I've got bitch tit. More on the left side than the right. It hurts all the time. I took Nolvadex and tamoxifen, but it didn't help, so I think it's just the way it's going to be. But I hate it. I hate taking off my shirt. For photo shoots I'll wet my nipple with spit so it'll look firm instead of hanging down like a little tit."

She leans forward and kisses me. Her hand finds my nipple. She kisses me there in my ugliness. She is gentle. It does not hurt the tenderness. I am dirty. She cleanses me. She pulls her lips away and looks up at me. She wants more.

"I got too big too fast and tore my hamstring, which destroyed my football career." Her fingers find the divot in the back of my leg. Then her lips. Kissing and kneading.

"All of my joints ache." Her lips are everywhere.

I stand up, turn to face her, and pull down my underwear. I'm standing naked in front of her.

"My . . . my balls . . . never really regained their size . . . they're kind of shriveled." Her lips are there, too.

She slips out of her jean skirt. "I want you to see me," she whispers, and lies back on the bed and splays herself open for me to see.

I suddenly understand her fascination with steroids, why she wants to know about the side effect. Why she is here.

"I took a lot of testost . . . and it caused . . . my clit—"

She isn't shy. She is serving herself up to me, not for sex, but for approval. *Look at me. Like me. Accept me. I'm damaged like you.*

"It caused . . . my clit to . . . grow."

I have sex with her, but it's awkward. I can feel her enlarged clit pressing against my pubic bone when I'm on top of her. I roll her over and take her from behind. It seems normal until she climbs onto all fours and I can see it sticking out from its little hood. It looks like a little baby's penis.

There's something oddly poetic about two broken people finding refuge in each other. Me with my swollen nipples and shriveled sac, and her with a clit the size of a small penis. Two people bonded in shame and sex by their secrets.

We lie in bed, postcoital, neither touching nor not touching. The awkwardness is gone. It is the still after sex. She is vulnerable and fragile. It is her turn to talk.

She tells me about her experience with steroids in pursuit of a bodybuilding title and how they eventually stripped her of everything feminine. At first it was the acne, and the facial peach fuzz that turned to whiskers. She found herself having to shave her chin and her upper lip, but it didn't really register with her because competitive bodybuilders shave all over. What was the big deal with having to shave one more place?

Then the hair on her head started to come out in clumps, but she never really noticed how thin it was because she was always adding extensions, to counter the hair loss. Then one day her hairstylist took her extensions out but wasn't able to put the new ones in until the following day. Angie went home that night, looked at herself in the mirror, and let out a silent scream. Her hair had thinned to the point where she looked like a cancer patient in the first stages of chemo. But this didn't stop her. She again rationalized the side effects, telling herself she would only stay on the Anavar testosterone cycle just a little longer.

It was always just a little longer.

Angie had a big contest coming up and believed if she placed well, it would change her life. She didn't place well, but her life was forever changed by the experience of steroids. Estrogen therapy slowly helped her reclaim *most* of the femininity that steroids had stripped from her. Her facial hair eventually disappeared, the hair on her head was thick and bountiful again, but the estrogen couldn't help her recover the ultimate symbol of womanhood.

The ability to create life.

To have a child.

Angie talks about her deep depression and the death of her womb. She talks about the heartache, the anger, the pain. We talk about suicide. What hurts Angie the most is that she was willing to make the choice. She willingly took the shots and swallowed the pills. Her own hand ripped the gift of motherhood from her. She says she couldn't help herself. She was swallowed by the obsession.

I tell her I have a son. Angie starts to weep. Even though she discovered her infertility years ago, the wound is still deep enough to cause her immense pain. She tells me how she can't even look at babies for a long time. She tells me she could be in love with me. She tells me to stop taking steroids.

I tell her, *Just a little longer.*

Her eyes search mine for a moment. Then she lies back, sad for my future.

I go to the set the next day, the overwhelming experience from the night before still fresh in my mind. I watch the female Gladiators as they warm up in the back room. Their chiseled muscles glisten as they stoke up their body's temperature with different exercises in preparation for the day's show. Rumors are floating around about steroid use among some of the women. They are huge, ripped, and athletic.

I study them, looking for signs of steroid use. I can see the beginning stages of masculinization in some of them. One of the first signs of steroid use in women is the loss of adipose (fatty) tissue in the face, making the features more pronounced, more male. Other signs are acne, facial hair, loss of breast tissue, lower voices. It goes on and on. They could all be on steroids . . . or they could all be natural and simply have more testosterone in their bodies. I don't know. I've never sold any of the girls, or injected any with, steroids. But I *do* know that a human body can only get so big naturally, and the men hate to kiss one female Gladiator "hello" because her razor stubble gives them whisker burn.

The show is about to start. The women Gladiators burst on the arena floor during their introduction. The crowd explodes. Still haunted by the overwhelming events of the night before, I can't

help but look at the female Gladiators and wonder if they're packing any secrets under their uniforms. I'm curious what their secrets
are. Their fears. Their shame.

Are they haunted?

Are they broken?

Do they silently promise themselves, *Just a little longer?*

CHAPTER 14

Oh, Shit!
I've Got Tits!

*B*itch tits, man boobs, breast-chesticles, is what they're called on the street. *Gynecomastia* is the scientific name. No matter what you call it, I have it.

I have tits.

The familiar mantra blasts through my head: *Something is not right.* But I store it in the file of things I've slowly become aware of, but don't do anything about.

My body is going through the feminization of breast tissue. This is thanks to an excess of estrogen in my body. The process is called aromatization. Androgens get converted to estrogen, which finds its way to the breast tissue. There it binds with the glandular tissue under the nipple, which hypertrophies. In simpler terms, your body senses there is too much testosterone in the system and produces estrogen in an effort to balance out your hormonal system. This extra estrogen causes you to grow breasts.

The initial tenderness soon turns into a lump around the nipple, which then turns into a sizable mass of tissue. This mass causes so much discomfort I can't hug anyone without hurting, and it's hideous-looking. Pumping up, dieting, and getting ripped only makes the problem worse because it highlights the protruding, budding breast on your chest. Most abusers suffer in silence and don't talk about it, but bitch tit can get so bad it can cause a man to lactate or secrete milk from his chest. One of the most startlingly freaky things I've seen is when a dark-haired, good-looking, massive kid lifted up his shirt to display his bitch tits. "Check this out," he said as he squeezed his nipple and out shot a stream of milk. He thought it was funny. I think he's an idiot.

Bitch tit doesn't happen to everyone who takes steroids. The more and the longer you take steroids, the greater the likelihood. To counteract the bitch tit effect, I take breast cancer drugs such as Nolvadex, Arimidex, and tamoxifen that I buy on the black market. Some reported complications of these estrogen-blocking drugs are vaginal bleeding, breast pain, blood clots, stroke, and abnormal growth of uterine tissue. Nice. And this is something I choose to take.

The tricky thing about bitch tit? It's most noticeable when I least want it to be. If the weather is cold, everything tightens up and it becomes less noticeable. But in warm take-my-shirt-off weather, my man boobs pout forward and I cannot hide them.

Secrecy is a steroid user's best friend. I don't want anyone to know I've used drugs to help obtain my mass and size. I want them to think I'm a freak of nature and got this godlike body through sheer hard work and determination. But steroid-induced bitch tits are the buds of truth sprouting out of my chest. I hate it. It feels like my body is betraying me, revealing the terrible lie I can't wash away or hide, a constant reminder glaring back at me in the mirror. But ultimately I see it as a necessary trade-off—which is what I'm always doing when I'm on a cycle. I'm making little deals with not only my conscience but also with my body. Slowly, through the Faustian arrangement, I end up giving pieces of myself away.

I notice my testicles are shriveling. It happens gradually. The first thing I become aware of is an ache in my balls after having sex. I know the tortured ache that comes from getting aroused and *not* having sex, but this dull, throbbing pain *after* sex is something new. I'm not alarmed. It simply registers, *Balls hurt after sex. Strange? Maybe it's because they're withering like raisins.* But I wipe the concern out of my mind because I don't want to attribute anything negative to taking steroids. I prefer to live with a little pain in my scrotum rather than to stop taking the drugs.

Then the strangest thing begins to happen.

One of my testicles starts disappearing during sex. The Mayo Clinic calls it a retractable testicle: the testicle doesn't stay in its proper position in the scrotum, but glides back and forth between the scrotum and the groin. I call it god-awful embarrassing. It happens near the moment of climax, when I clench my muscles tight, trying to see God, then *fww-iip*! It's gone and I've only got one marble in the sack. I know it sounds really fucking weird, and even as I write this, it still seems a bit surreal. It reminds me of a scene from an early Woody Allen movie.

"Houston . . . we have a problem."

A horde of white-clad mad scientists rush to the control panel. "This is Houston. Say again?"

"Houston, I said, we have a problem." A prolonged dramatic pause, then the radio squelches, "Houston . . . Nitro is missing a nut."

There's a mad scramble as scientists go into frantic action searching for the free-floating orb lost somewhere in the universe of my scrotum. They send out tiny, little men in white suits who shoot into my scrotum to retrieve the missing ball.

I'm making light of a sick, serious situation, but how in the hell else do you wrap your mind around the fact that during sex you lose a testicle? This is something I chose to do to myself over and over. And the new drugs I take to combat the situation are no longer derived from pregnant women's piss. They are heavy-duty anticancer drugs for women with breast cancer. So, I've gone from using pregnancy-hormone-drenched piss to medicine meant to cure breast cancer.

Pretty cool, huh?

Houston . . . we have a problem.

Nitro is out of his fucking mind.

I discover some good news about gynecomastia. It's reversible, but only through surgery. The procedure costs close to $10,000, which leaves me on the outside looking in. During the first half of season one of the *Gladiators*, my uniform consists of two bolero sequin straps that crisscross my chest to form an X. But the swath of cloth that crosses my chest and covers my nipple isn't wide enough to cover the outer portion of my pec, thus exposing the small lumps underneath the sheath of muscle. It is a constant struggle pulling the strap over trying to hide the man boobs. I don't know if anyone notices, but to me, I feel like that is all people see when they look at me.

When the first half of the season is over, I plead with the wardrobe stylist to make me a new uniform. I can't tell her it is to hide my budding breasts, so I make up a lie—the straps kept falling off during competition, and I'd be able to kick more ass if I didn't have to bother with the stupid straps. Now, though, the situation is way beyond a costume change, and I see I have to do something about it. The first break we get, I pay a visit to a plastic surgeon.

Santa Monica is a sleepy ocean town, void of smog, where there's always a gentle breeze. A few tall building sprinkle the landscape to remind you that even though it's relaxed, business is still done here.

I walk into the plastic surgeon's office ready to meet Dr. Thompson, an extremely pleasant but not a phony man, relaxed yet serious enough to make you feel comfortable that he can get the job done. I dive right in. "Doc, I've been taking steroids for years and I've got gynecomastia. I hate it. I'm embarrassed to take my shirt off. It's painful, and I want you to fix it."

"Let's talk about your medical his—"

"Doc, can you fix it or not?" I interrupt.

He calmly looks me in the eye. "Yes, I can."

I feel an immediate wave of relief pass over me and I relax back in my chair. He has said the magic words and now I will listen or do anything he needs me to. Dr. Thompson examines my chest, pressing on the area around my nipples. He asks if it's painful.

"Uncomfortable, not painful," I say.

Dr. Thompson gently squeezes my left nipple between his thumb and first finger.

"Oww!" I yell, and jerk back.

"It's a bit tender and there is a considerable-sized hard mass present."

Considerable? Compared to what?

The doctor looks at me squarely and says, "Dan, I'm going to need to get a mammogram to determine how much fat and glandular tissue your chest contains. There's a very small possibility that it's cancerous."

"*Cancer?*" I exhale audibly.

"Yes, there's always the possibility that the growths can be tumors."

The word *cancer* makes me instantly humble and scared. I thought this was just a humiliating side effect of steroids.

"How will we know if it's cancerous or not?" I ask.

"During the procedure we'll take a biopsy of the mass we excise and send it to the lab." Dr. Thompson must've seen the scared look on my face because he quickly reassured me it was very unlikely and said, "The good news is that because there is the possibility of its being cancerous, I might be able to get your insurance to cover it."

To hell with the insurance covering it, I just don't want this to be cancer.

His assistant leads me to the X-ray room and tells me to sit in the chair in front of a five-foot-high, rectangular-looking machine with a giant viselike arm. She instructs me to lean forward and put the left breast into the vise, saying, "This may be a little uncomfortable." The machine starts to whir and the vise slowly clamps down on my chest. "Compression is necessary to hold the breast still to avoid blurring of the image and to even up the breast thickness so all the breast tissue can be visualized."

I dislike this woman. She keeps calling my chest a *breast*. Maybe she doesn't know I'm Nitro. That I bench five hundred pounds. That I played professional football . . . that . . .

The machine clicks. The mechanical sound catches me off guard.

"Put your right breast in the machine please."

Damn it. There she goes again calling my chest a *breast*. I'm just about to correct her when I realize that I'm what's out of place. I'm the one who's in the doctor's office getting a mammogram that is used specifically to screen breast disease in women. This woman is simply doing her job the way she does every day.

After a couple more X-rays, she leads me back to Dr. Thompson. He says the procedure will be done with me as an outpatient and will take two hours. They're going to make a one-inch incision at the bottom of my areola and excise the mass. Then they will liposuction the fatty tissue out and try to contour the area so the nipples will sit right on my chest.

"Will the scars be visible?" I ask.

"There will be some discoloration," the doctor says, "but if I do my job right, there won't be much of a scar. Still, I have to make you aware of possible complications with this procedure."

"Like what? My nipple will explode?" I say, trying to add some levity.

Dr. Thompson adjusts his glasses and doesn't laugh. I understand that he can't make jokes about the complications, because it's a doctor's duty to inform his patients of complications. If he doesn't, he could be setting himself up for a possible malpractice lawsuit.

"But, Your Honor, he never told me *my nipple could explode!*"

Dr. Thompson says he'll do his best to contour the area, but I could be left with an indentation in my nipple. I could also lose all sensation in my nipples, and in rare occurrences the nipple placement could be different. He went on with a laundry list of other possible complications. Hematoma, excessive bleeding, blood clotting, heavy scarring, recurrence of breast tissue. And the general precautions about anesthesia—heart attack and stroke.

I shudder. I haven't fully admitted the severity of the operation to myself. I thought it'd be easy, he'd just go in and do a little nip and stitch. But the thing that frightens me the most is that I won't be able to work out for four to six weeks. To me, it's a lifetime.

The day of the operation arrives quickly. "Count backwards from one hundred," the anesthesiologist says as she leans over me. I'm suddenly afraid. I search my mind for answers. Where in the hell is this reluctance, this fear, coming from?

It hits me. The last time I had surgery, they told me I'd be back playing in a couple of weeks and then I woke up with a cast on my leg and was out for the season. That surgery led me down the road to steroids. With that surgery, hell began. I start to wonder how different my life might have been if I'd never taken a steroid. I start to think about my purpose in life. Why am I here? What am I supposed to do? I start to think about my brother. I try to push the thoughts of *him* out of my head. I think of him every day . . . and yet I don't think of him. I don't allow myself. But the thoughts of him are pushing their way forward with a desperate urgency. Push it away. Push it all away. In an instant, I'm back in Vietnam . . .

———

I'm ten years old. I'm with my stepmother, Kimm. We're walking through a cemetery in the black of night. I'm scared. I want to hold her hand, but my anger and revulsion toward her is stronger than the fear. She is leading me somewhere, pushing me along until we're standing in front of a small room in a building. It's concrete, cold and austere. A morgue. She shuttles me through the door. I'm almost knocked off my feet by the stinging odor of formaldehyde, but it's still not strong enough to cover the dank smell of death. The room is lined with sliding storage drawers stacked three high. Kimm mumbles something to a technician. He slides a drawer open, revealing my dead brother. His body is rigid, frozen, and covered in a sheen of frost that makes him appear as though he's made of plaster. I crumble to my knees and look up at her, tears in my eyes. "WHY?! WHY DID YOU TAKE ME HERE?!"

Kimm's face turns into an ugly sneer. "I wanted you to see what your father did." She laughs a shrill, reverberating laugh that turns to a hideous cackle.

I snap out of the memory with a scream. I jerk upright and yell at the nurse, "Wait! I don't want to do this!" Suddenly hands are all over me, holding me down.

"Stay down!" a voice hollers.

"Let go of me! I'm not doing this!"

"Dr. Thompson!" someone yells.

Seconds later he rushes over to me. "Dan, what's the matter?"

"I can't do this, Dr. Thompson. I'm sorry . . . I just can't." I plead with him on the verge of tears, "Please . . . please don't make me do it."

He gently places a hand on my shoulder. "Dan, we're already done. You're in the recovery room."

I close my eyes and fade back into the black, bottomless anesthetic sleep.

A few hours later I'm home, lying on my bed, wearing a bra-like corset that covers the top of my chest to the bottom of my abdomen. One-inch-long drainage tubes jut out from each nipple, into glass ampoules that I have to change out every few hours when they fill with blood. I'm still fighting the haze of anesthesia, and I'm hungry but too nauseated to get up and grab a bite of food.

I am alone. That's the way I like it. I don't want anyone having to depend on me and I don't want to depend on anyone either. I know it's about fear—of wanting, needing someone, then having the person not be there. Since my brother died, I've learned not to count on or need anyone but myself.

I wake up later that morning and stand, corset off, in front of the mirror, looking at my scarred container of a body, wrapped in bloody gauze. As I unwind the gauze, I can feel the fabric sticking to the drainage ampoules and realize that the tubes must have overflowed while I was asleep. I suddenly remember Dr. Thompson telling me I need to change the ampoules every few hours and, even though he had to remove a lot of tissue, it wasn't cancerous.

I stare at my reflection in the mirror. I exhale deeply, fighting back the nausea, fatigue, pain. My chest is black-and-blue, swollen, covered in dried blood with tubes, ampoules. My nipples are zippered with black stitches. I look worn, beaten, old. As I take a damp cloth and wipe off the dried blood, I feel a giant blast of anger. I'm mad. Mad at having stitches in my chest, mad at having blood caked across me, mad at the damn blood-filled ampoules, mad at being *alone*. Mad at the *lie*.

If steroids made me into such a man, then how come I had to get breast tissue removed from my chest?

Standing there, I promise myself, *I'll never take another steroid.*

I say it again: *I'm never taking steroids.*

I repeat it a third time: *I'm never taking steroids.*

I know I'm trying to convince myself because I know the truth. *I'm not going to quit.*

CHAPTER 15

Drug Tests:
They Really Don't Want to Know

I drive through the morning calm on a pearl gray Saturday to meet
the producers of *American Gladiators*. Production isn't scheduled
to start for a few months, so this meeting with all the Gladiators is
highly unusual. The Samuel Goldwyn Company doesn't normally
like all of the Gladiators to get together outside the show. It usually
leads to a revolt where we ask for a raise or better food or some
other perk.

We revolted during season two as the show first started
becoming a hit. We were on billboards, countless magazine covers,
and were only getting paid union minimum. We asked for a small
raise and they said no. So all ten Gladiators got together and
walked out in the middle of production. They threatened to fire
and sue us. But we had strength in solidarity and we knew we had
them by the balls. I only wished we had grabbed them by the jugu-
lar and asked for more money. Sam Goldwyn, head of Samuel
Goldwyn Company, is notoriously tightfisted and acted like we

were taking food off his table when our walkout resulted in the Gladiators getting a raise from $700 an episode to $1,000 an episode.

So, here we are, big television stars making a whopping $26,000 a year. I hop out of the car, step into the Los Angeles heat, and say hello to a few of the other Gladiators who are waiting outside the two-story brick building. A nervous energy is in the air. We're all thinking the same thing. Why have they summoned us here? Something has to be up.

The ten of us huddle into a small, pale room and wait for the producer to show up. A few minutes later he enters the room with a dire look on his face. A pall falls across the room like someone has died. My first thought is *Oh, shit, they've canceled the show.*

The producer stands at the front of the room and says, "I've got some bad news for you."

My heart sinks. This is it. The show is done. My mind starts to race. How will I make a living? Maybe I'll try WWF or get into the broadcasting booth somewhere and try hosting. Deep in survival mode, I start to calculate how much money I've saved up from my appearances and how long it will last.

The producer continues, "Because of this Hulk Hogan / Vince McMahon WWF steroid scandal, we're getting crucified in the press about the possibility of members on this show using steroids. That's not an image we want to project. A lot of kids watch this show and we're getting pressures from our sponsors to drug-test you guys."

My heart starts to pound in my chest triple time. I panic. A drug test? A fucking drug test? There is absolutely no way I can pass a drug test.

The producer continues, "If steroids or any other illegal drugs are detected in your drug test, you will be immediately terminated."

A stunned silence fills the room. The blood drains out of almost everyone's face as we see our careers flash before our eyes.

I am suddenly aware of how sterile the room is, with its fluorescent lights and white tile floors. It could pass for a medical clinic. A new flush of panic runs through me. *Oh, shit, they're going to test us right here on the spot.* I know they can't force us to take the test, but by not taking it, isn't that indirectly admitting your guilt?

I raise my hand and ask, trying to sound as casual as possible, "When are we getting tested?"

"We're scheduling it now. We'll be contacting you to let you know."

The room loosens up and we breathe a collective sigh of relief. Having even twenty-four hours before the test will make a difference. Supposedly a multitude of masking agents can hide the use of drugs. I'm sure I can get my hands on them. I have to. I have a lot to hide.

Steroids aren't the only drugs I'm using. I use other drugs to relieve the pressure of using steroids. With steroids, my motor runs so fast, I have to find a way to let out the steam or I'm going to perpetually have my hands around someone's neck, trying to choke the life out of him.

After the meeting, I rush home, consumed with thoughts of how to pass the drug test. I call a few of my bodybuilding buddies up at Gold's Gym North Hollywood and tell them I need something to beat a drug test. I'm stunned to discover they don't have anything. They all say, "Bodybuilders aren't tested for 'roids, so we don't need anything."

I try to call Dr. Kerr, the doctor who gave me my first cycle over ten years ago, but his number is disconnected. After asking around, I learn he is being incarcerated by the Feds for the distribution of steroids. Great. I'm so fired.

I go to the local library in hopes of uncovering some evidence on how long certain drugs stay in your system. I don't get concrete facts, just estimates, depending on the particular test and usage. Regardless, the discovery isn't good news.

Deca-Durabolin: 1 year

Testosterone cypionate: 3–6 months

Marijuana: depends

Dianabol: 3 months

Anavar: 2 months

GUILTY. GUILTY. GUILTY. GUILTY. GUILTY.

I've always heard that drug tests are a joke because, if you're smart enough, there's a way to beat them. I'm pretty smart when it comes to steroid pharmacology, but I don't have any idea how to beat this drug test. All of the so-called masking agents are elusive. None of the so-called experts and doctors know how to beat the test in such a short time. Which, of course, makes sense. If drug tests are so easy to beat and masking agents are so readily available, then how come so many wealthy, prominent athletes fail drug tests?

I pace my living room in a panic. I just won't answer my phone. I figure if the producers can't find me, they can't test me. The phone rings later that evening. It's the producers from the show. I don't answer it. They call again the next morning. I still don't answer it. My agent calls that afternoon. Like an idiot, I answer, thinking he may have a movie role for me. My agent tells me the Gladiators are having a mandatory meeting at the end of the week and I have to be there. I tell him I'm not going. He tells me I have to. That's what *mandatory* means.

"Tell them I'm outta town."

"But you're not."

"Lie for me."

"Can't do that."

"But you're an agent. Isn't that what you do?"

"I have to tell them I reached you. It's up to you to go to the meeting or not."

"Jeez. Thanks."

Out of all the agents in Hollywood, I have to have the only honest one.

———

It's four days before D-day. Four days before my life will explode. I meet with a nutritionist friend of mine. She tells me the best chance I have to beat the test is to flush out my system. She recommends the Master Cleanse fast. You consume nothing but a quart of warm salt water followed by a watered mixture of maple syrup, lemon juice, and cayenne pepper, all day until the day of the test. That's four days. That's forever.

I normally eat seventy-five hundred calories a day, divided into meals every three hours. Just the thought of not being able to eat makes me hungry. Everything starts to look like food. But that isn't the worst part. She says that to give myself a fighting chance at actually flushing my system in four short days, I also have to get a colonic.

Colonic. I don't even like the sound of the word.

"What's a colonic?" I ask.

"It's a process where they stick a small tube into your anus and—"

"Whoa, whoa. Back up. They stick a tube where?"

"Up your anus."

I chew on the word for a second. *Anus.* I feel the need to clarify. "You mean up my butt?"

"Yes, they stick a tube up your rectum and shoot a stream of water into your colon. A second tube goes in there, too, that sucks out the water and fecal matter."

The blood drains from my face. Two tubes in my rectum? It *isn't* going to happen. I once broke up with a hot Brazilian chick, Mara, after she continually tried to stick a finger in my rear during sex. She managed to sneak the tip of her finger in there once and I scooted across the room like a bottle rocket. I look at the nutritionist. She's giggling.

"Am I missing something? Is something funny here?"

"Oh, you macho guys always get so weirded out when it

comes to your poop-pinchers. It's a perfectly natural and healthy process."

Poop-pincher? Did she just say *poop-pincher?* I know we're friends but she just crossed the line. This isn't a joking matter. I abruptly stand and say, "Just give me the card of the person who does it and I'll be on my way."

I drive straight to the colonic center in Beverly Hills and enter the plush office. I approach the reception desk only to be greeted by, not one, but three extremely attractive receptionists. "Good afternoon. How can we help you?" they say in unison.

"I'm here to get a . . . a . . ." I can't even get myself to say it.

"A colonic?" one of the women asks.

I nod, trying to hold on to a speck of dignity.

"Don't worry about it. It's a perfectly natural and healthy process," they say with Stepford-wife smiles.

"So I'm told."

"Just fill out these forms and Olga will be with you shortly."

Olga? Did she just say *Olga?* The very name conjures up horrible images. I figure it's the old bait and switch. They butter you up with these three beauties, only to turn you over to have your ass raped by an Eastern Bloc bruiser named Olga.

Ten minutes later a door to a room opens and a massive mountain of a woman calls out my name in a thick German accent. It's Olga and she doesn't disappoint. She is every bit of six foot two and weighs 250. Her frame fills the door and blocks out the light. I only see her in silhouette—and when I do, a tiny tear escapes from the corner of my eye.

In a stiff-hand gesture reminiscent of Hitler, she directs me to enter the room. It feels like I'm being led to the gallows. I half expect the Stepford receptionists to holler out, "Dead man walking!" or "Fresh meat."

Olga closes the door behind her. She tosses a smock at me. "You undress now."

I look for a curtain or some other type of shelter to change behind, but there's nothing. A stiff, laminate table is the centerpiece that dominates the room. Beside it is a futuristic-looking tank-of-a-machine, covered in blinking lights, knobs, and buttons with sinewy tubes jutting out its sides like arms. It looks like something you'd see in an episode of *Get Smart* or *Lost in Space*.

I strip naked and slip on the smock. Olga watches me every second of the way as I feel my penis shrink to embarrassing proportions. I slide onto the table and lie on my back. The veneer top is freezing. My penis shrinks even smaller. Olga orders me to lift my legs and feet up into a "birthing" position. My smock forms a tent held up by my knees with shriveled penis being the center point.

Olga disappears into the tent and I don't think I've ever felt more vulnerable in my life. Seconds later she commands me, "Relax," and I feel something huge trying to invade my sphincter. I jerk straight up into a sitting position. "What the hell are you trying to put up there?!"

Olga emerges from the tent, holding something that looks no bigger than the tip of a Water Pik toothbrush.

"That's it? It felt like you were trying to stick a fire hose up there."

"You very tight," she says in her thick accent.

For some reason, this makes me beam with pride. But the pride turns to horror when she reaches for the K-Y jelly and disappears back underneath the tent. The next thing you know, I feel her lubing up my most private place. "You need to relax" are her last words.

Then it happens.

Penetration.

I know it's only four skinny Water Pik inches, but it feels like the Alaskan pipeline is being laid in my rectum. Next comes the tube to suck out the fecal matter. Now water is being shot inside my colon. I stifle a scream. Olga calls me "a little baby." I don't know if she said this because I'm acting like an infant or because my penis has shrunk even more.

Olga flips a switch. Red and green lights flash on top of the machine as the clear-plastic, shit-sucking tube that runs from my rectum to the machine slowly fills with water. Moments later, it's *ka-chunk. Ka-chunk. Ka-chunk.* Brown particles float through the tube. Olga has the uncanny ability to identify the free-floating fecal asteroids: "I see you eat broccoli last night. Hmm, you should chew your corn better." When something pink and rubbery floats by, she says, "Don't swallow your gum. It's not healthy."

I tell her I haven't had gum since I was a kid.

Her face breaks into a tight-lipped grin. "Exactly."

After about thirty minutes, the water in the tube is once again clear. I relax, believing it must be over. But Olga reaches under the tent and wrenches the Water Pik tube in a grinding, circular motion. "You must clean sides, too," she says.

Ka-chunk. Ka-chunk. Ka-chunk.

She's right. Fecal matter clings to the sides of my colon.

Finally it's over. She pulls the tubes out and orders me to go to the toilet. I tell her I'll wait until I get home.

"There's much water in you. You go now."

I don't feel anything and repeat that I can wait. "Remember, you said I was tight," I say proudly. I slip my clothes on and start heading to the door, when my stomach rumbles. *Gruuu-mmp. Gruuu-uuump.* I look at Olga in a mad panic. She points to the bathroom. I race inside and tear my pants down as a tidal wave of water rushes out of me in loud, gushing gasps and wallops that sound like a car crash. After ten noisy, gut-busting minutes, I emerge from the bathroom directly into the lobby. As I exit, I notice everyone staring at me. I lower my head and walk out, trying to preserve any dignity I might have left.

I return home. Anything left in my colon I flush out over the next two days with the lemon juice, maple syrup, and cayenne concoction. I won't go into more details, except to say that the colors and gunk that come out of me make the rainbow Play-Doh specialty pack look bland.

Friday finally arrives. I've lost twelve pounds in four days. I feel like the incredible shrinking man with a horrible caffeine-withdrawal headache on the way to the drug test. I chug the gallon of cranberry juice my nutritionist suggested. I'm tired, cranky, and haven't eaten in four days. But as I enter the building, I feel I've done everything I can to pass the test in the short time.

When I walk inside, the producer gathers us in the same room as before. He steps to the front of the group and says his perfunctory hellos. *Just cut through the shit. Let's get this thing started so I can go eat a decent meal.* He continues gabbing about different pieces of business. I can barely focus on him I'm so famished from not eating.

"Okay, we've got a date for the drug test," he says.

A thick silence fills the room.

"We'll be testing you in six weeks."

A sense of relief washes over me. There is an audible collective sigh. I'll be living to fight another day. As fun as *Gladiators* is, at the end of the day it is a job. It's my livelihood, and taking steroids is just part of the job. I always thought some of the producers knew about the steroids, the same way management in baseball must know.

I come to the stark realization that, just as in baseball and other professional sports, some of the producers of the *Gladiators* are not only willing to look the other way when it comes to steroid use, they are willing to do what is necessary to protect their property. Unlike cocaine, which devalues the producer's property, steroids actually help—at least in the short term. When home runs are sailing over fences and bodies are flying around in the gladiator arena, the ratings go up and the revenue comes in. The producers have a good reason to look the other way. By giving us the test dates in advance, they are doing more than ignoring the evidence. They're implicitly giving us a chance to come off the drugs and pass the test. It's symptomatic of a fast-growing cancer in sports and entertainment in this country, where we gladly sell our morals for a paycheck.

During the clean period, when I take off the meat-suit, I feel the first inklings of something scratching at the window of my soul wanting to be let out. But this knocking of humanity on the door of my subconscious will have to wait. It isn't time. I'm so wrapped up in the moment, I choke it back, suffocating and obliterating it into a black pool in my subconscious. But it's too late . . . the damage is done and traces of life and humanness are scattered across the landscape of my psyche like speed bumps on a road.

We all take the drug test six weeks later. I have no idea who passes or who fails. To this day, I still don't have a clue. They never tell us or anyone else. But at the start of the next season, the show announces to the American public, "The Gladiators have all been drug-tested!" The day after the test, I hop back on the steroid train, on a collision course with destiny—on a collision course with myself.

Backstage with Jim Starr (Laser) and
Steve Henneberry (Tower).

Me at the age of one
in Japan.

My mother and father in Japan in 1963.

The last photo of Randy,
Christine, and me together.

My hero, my idol, my best friend: my brother Randy with a protective arm slung over my shoulder.

(Left to right) Me, Christine, Debbie, Michelle, and Kevin—all of my siblings except for my younger brother John-John.

After a Santa Ana JC football game with my stepdad John, my father Wally, and Christine; with Kevin and Michelle in front.

Nice mustache I'm sporting in my SJSU Spartan uniform.

Condo in cleats: I'm the big hunk of beef, number 95, playing in the Italian Super Bowl.

My beautiful baby boy, Tyler.

Walking on clouds at the Haleakala Crater in Maui.

Some of the crazy jobs I did for money
when I first got to Hollywood!

Goofing around
with Lace.

At the Dallas Reunion Arena.
The tour was out of control.

I've been plasticized.

The creator of *American Gladiators*
Johnny Ferraro and I backstage.
The other creator, Dan Carr, is
not shown.

With a very special
Gladiator fan.

I always made sure to
sign every autograph.

Shooting a commercial with my son, Tyler.

This is how the big kids do it.

A fan favorite, the Assault.

Me with Mike Adamle, Gemini (I call him Big Mike), and Larry Csonka.

Season seven. I ditched the spandex and cohosted the show. I'm with my brother Kevin.

Speaking to a group of kids.

CHAPTER 16

Playboy Bunnies,
Porn Stars, and Strippers

Everyone *thinks* it would be great to have sex with a porn star. Well, let me tell you something . . .

It is.

I first meet Amber at the Hollywood Tropicana, a mud-wrestling palace of decadence where famous Hollywood pussy hounds patrol. While Joe from Iowa and Bob from Kentucky fork over their hard-earned dough to roll in the mud with one of these bronzed bikini beauties, my friends and I come here with the intention of pulling a couple of girls out of the club to go partying for the night. On one of these fishing expeditions, I land Amber, a former porn star. She's a stunning, petite blonde with a squeaky voice, who is sorrowful, sexy, and elegant all at once.

The great thing about having sex with a porn star is there is no uncharted territory. You can pretty much do whatever you want. There are no horrified exclamations of "You want to put what where???" There is never a "You bastard" look after you bring up the idea of throwing another girl into the mix. Instead it's "Which girlfriend should I call?" But the biggest lesson I learn from my experiences with porn stars and strippers is that most of them are *broken.* Daddy issues, incest, abuse, drugs. All I have to do is look past Amber's megakilowatt smile and into her eyes. There, I can see the damage and pain. I can see the shame. It isn't something a man can heal. It has to heal from within, and at this time in my life I'm not in the healing business.

I'm in the business of the hyperexperience. To feel anything at all—pleasure or pain—sex by itself isn't enough. I need to have sex with a porn star or Playboy bunny or film myself fucking a girl. I have sex with a girl just because she's a squirter. I hook up with another porn star because I like to watch movies of her getting plowed, then have sex with her while the pornographic images run through my head like a freight train.

But it hasn't always been like this.

I grew up adoring women. In kindergarten I'd lie near the doorway during naptime with the reckless hope of getting a peek up my teacher's dress when she walked over me. At home when a commercial of a woman showering was on TV and they would only show the top of her chest and up, I'd walk up to the screen, press my chubby, six-year-old face against the glass, then look down trying to see rest of her naked body.

I see my first naked girl when I'm ten. But she isn't a regular girl. She is a prostitute. It's when I am living in Vietnam with my father. She is one of his tea girls. I remember it like it was yesterday.

I'm standing on the balcony of my bedroom. The tea girls' dressing room is across the courtyard and one story below. I can see her enter the room through a generous opening in the window curtain. She is beautiful and young with almond eyes and thick, black hair. My first thought is, she doesn't belong here and has taken a wrong turn on the way to school or she is here visiting her sister or mother. But then she unbuttons her silk blouse, exposing the breasts of a woman that seem mercilessly too large for her frail body. Her fingers find the buttons of her skirt. She begins unsnapping them, then suddenly stops, aware she is being watched. After a long moment she looks up at me. The blood shotguns to my head so fast I can barely stand as she continues to undress, her eyes never leaving mine. I'm hard in an instant, filled with feelings I've never experienced before. It's a mad rush of desire, agony, lust, and pain. It is overwhelming.

I think it's love. I know now it's the *fever*.

The other tea girls tease me endlessly. "Boss's son, you cherry boy? You want to lose your cherry?" I do want to have sex, but only with her. I know, but I don't really comprehend, she's a whore. I think I'm in love with her. I save money to give to her. I want her to have a better life.

I am a fool at ten years old and I'm a fool at thirty-seven when my wife assures me her coworker and her are just *friends*. Six months later we divorce, then shortly after that they marry. I have the fever, but women have the power.

I used to be paralyzed by a woman's beauty.

And a slave to it. But through years of experience, I've found the more attractive the girl, usually the worse she is in bed.

The truth is, beautiful girls cannot fuck.

They lead with their beauty instead of their heart, soul, and flesh. You can't fuck beauty. You can only adore it and objectify it. I want to bust through the facade. Beautiful women are the ultimate poseurs. They aren't able to free themselves from their own observation and are ultimately unable to give themselves to a partner.

Throughout my teen years, I'm filled with the fever. I'm locked, loaded, ready to fire. But it takes a few years and hundreds of rejections before I actually have sex with a girl. I still have to shed the baby fat. I still have to become something remotely desirable. This happens when I am fourteen. I rise out of the ashes and sprout up to nearly six feet tall. The tub of fat around my stomach disappears and suddenly I'm a man. Lisa Rawlings, the neighborhood good-time girl, finds me desirable enough. She is a cute brunette, too cute, to be just giving it away the way she is. We cut school my sophomore year and sneak off to my house to hang out by the pool. She slides into a bikini while I rifle through my dad's medicine cabinet pilfering a couple of Valiums.

I slip a pill in her mouth.

Twenty minutes later, I'm *in* her.

On a weight bench, in the middle of an idyllic Wednesday afternoon, Lisa ruins me. After we finish—which takes longer than I expect for my first time because of the Valium—she slides down and sucks me off. I think this is the normal progression of the sex sequence. I think it is always going to be this way. I spend a lotta time on the bench over the years, but never again like I did with Lisa Rawlings.

Now that I'm in the club, my confidence soars, but it still takes a year to find another willing participant.

Her name is Jessica. She has a face that could stop a runaway bus and braces that could mangle, but all I care about are her oversized, blossoming breasts and her too tight rocker pants that show everything. The best thing about Jessica is that she says yes at a party when I ask her to go out to the backseat of my car.

After Jessica, I'm on a roll. I am flush with the fever and completely consumed with having sex. Every attractive girl I meet, all I think about is how to get into her pants. I spend a lot of time trying, but not much time actually doing it until my senior year in high school.

My first steady sexual partner is Jenny, a crushingly attractive head cheerleader at my high school. We're both seniors. This is my first consistent sex, where I don't feel in a rush and I have a chance to explore the beauty that is the female body. It only makes me want sex more. I want it all the time. *All the time*. I have sex with

Jenny in the bathroom at my dad's house while she is on her period, during Thanksgiving dinner. She lifts a leg up on the sink. I enter and thrust away. Blood drips on the floor while my relatives stuff their faces with turkey.

Being with girls and playing sports are the only ways I know how to feel good about myself. They are both outward manifestations that I am somebody.

At the end of my senior year when I break up with Jenny, she lies on the floor in the corner of her bedroom in the fetal position, weeping. I can see her pain and desperation, but I'm so detached from the situation, it's like I'm watching a movie. I don't understand the outpour of emotion. I don't know she has dreams regarding our future. I don't know she has put so much of her hope and life into me. I did spend my entire senior year of high school with her, I did grow close to her mother, and I did tell her I loved her. But in the relationship, I am only a visitor. I want to be there, but I don't know how. All I know is Jenny is crying, it is uncomfortable, so I stand up and walk out.

This will become a pattern over the years. I will date a girl for eight to twelve months but never longer than a year. As soon as the romance and fun fade, as soon as it gets uncomfortable, I'm gone.

After my brother's death, I'm not going to allow myself to invest in someone else. It's not a conscious choice. It is survival. Love is just a vestigial word for a feeling I've never felt.

In my senior yearbook, on the posterity page, when I am asked to predict where I'll be in ten years, I write something like "Living in France and being a gigolo." That's how absurd I am. And the entire time I think I am so much cooler than people who are actually building a life.

With celebrity comes a whole new world of decadence and indulgence. If college, football, and Italy opened up the floodgates, then *Gladiators* is a veritable tsunami. Life becomes an all-you-can-eat buffet of women, drugs, and partying. They come in all colors, sizes, and shapes. They are strippers, Playboy bunnies, actresses, models . . . But the onslaught just becomes a parade of faceless women, endless nights, interchangeable parties and drugs. Everything is always changing, but always the same. It becomes hard to tell where a night with one girl ends and a day with the next girl begins. One day blends into the next day until it is five thousand colliding days. Everything is a blur.

I don't remember the specifics of a lot of these encounters. I'd love to give you numbers because that's what guys always ask, but I simply do not remember with enough clarity to give an accurate account.

Case in point. Recently, while having dinner with my friend Brian at his restaurant Rosie's New York Pizza in San Jose, he tells me one of the best weeks of his life was when we took a trip to Mazatlán, Mexico, during spring break.

"Yeah, yeah, I remember that trip. There was a girl in the Jacuzzi or something like that," I say.

Brian throws a hard glance at me. "What do you mean 'something like that'? We tore up that town." He tells me about a crazy trip, a ménage à trois, rip-roaring sexual encounters, day and night. It all sounds great to me, and I'm sure I enjoyed it. I just don't remember it.

I do remember falling asleep while having sex with a girl and waking up to her cursing and slapping me. I remember my favorite pickup line from a girl: "My girlfriend and I would like to take you home."

I also remember the Playboy bunny who came over to my house with black-and-blue bruises around her eyes and bandages across her nose from a nose job. She wanted to have sex and I wouldn't touch her. In contrast, I remember another bunny who showed up with bandages on her new, huge breasts from a boob job whom I *did* want to have sex with, but she wouldn't let me do anything but squeeze them.

I could never forget my cute blond neighbor who knocked on my door in her cutoff shorts and said, "My friend wants to fuck you." While I did, my neighbor barked out sexual orders like "Give it to her harder," "Thrust deeper," and "Make her beg for it."

I also recall running into my grade-school fantasy Janet Jenson, who back then was distant and unattainable. I did what I couldn't do twenty years earlier. I had her. But sadly she was just a shadow of her former self, ravaged by alcohol and divorce. There was no satisfaction or joy in our coupling. It was a futile attempt to grasp at something I should've left in the past.

Above all else, I do *clearly* remember the ten or so girls who really meant something to me.

On steroids, I'm not 235 pounds of impotent, nonfucking flesh. I have sex. A lot of sex. Whether I limp my way through at half-mast or fight on proudly full steam ahead, I always fight the fight whenever I can. But I'm always on opposite ends of the pendulum. I either have a girl bent over the hood of my car on the side of the freeway, having sex with her as traffic blares by, or I'm lying in bed jerking off, sweating, trying to get hard for the girl next to me who is willing and waiting. That's just the way it is.

I want to please. I have to perform. I want to shine.

But with celebrity everything changes. Except nothing really changes. Because wherever I go—there I am.

And I am a man hiding in plain sight pretending to be a human being.

CHAPTER 17

I've Been Plasticized!

American Gladiators is blowing up. In some markets, *Gladiators* draws more viewers than pro baseball and basketball broadcasts. In other markets *Gladiators* gets higher ratings than the National Football League. We are the top-rated new syndicated show. We're plastered all over the media and on billboards across the country. It strikes a chord in the hearts of Americans. *American Gladiators* is a smash hit.

A press agent says, "It seems like there are fewer and fewer opportunities to find out who you really are. With this combination of violence and discipline—brains and brawn—you have a hell of a way to find out. Same thing from the fans' perspective. There's no BS. Two guys are stripped down. One wins, one loses. Where else do you get that anymore?"

So here's why it works:

The show is entertaining, lighthearted, and full of action. It has pro wrestling with all the glamour and the muscles, but we throw in normal people to prove it isn't scripted. It helps people forget about mundane, entry-level jobs. It gives every weekend warrior a chance to prove his mettle against superhero athletes. It quenches the thirst everyone has for his or her fifteen minutes of fame. It gives people sitting at home watching the show who think, "Hey, I can do that," a chance to put their money where their mouth is, to come on the show and compete.

You add an awesome Bill *Rocky* Conti theme song. You incorporate elements from other sports—football, most prominently— that give it athletic familiarity. And every single week you have the most important factor in any compelling sports competition—an underdog in the form of that week's victim or . . . uh, "contestant."

> Says gladiator Dan Clark, better known as Nitro: "For the spellers, you've got *Wheel of Fortune*; for the guys who go shopping, you've got *The Price Is Right*; for the athlete, you've got *American Gladiators*."
>
> —*Time* magazine

As Gladiators, we care about the outcome of every event and gave it our all each and every time. It means something to us. We are honored to wear the colors of our country and carry the spirit of our great nation in our hearts. It is raw and savage. It is profoundly American. President Bill Clinton says his favorite show during his White House days was *American Gladiators*, which he and his daughter, Chelsea, always watched. It is an arena in which any man or woman who works hard has a chance to make his or her dreams come true.

Critics think it's another signpost on the road to the apocalypse. They think *Gladiators* is a watershed for everything that is bad about TV, the media, and our obsession with fame. But we have a husband-and-wife team who both get on the show and call it the best vacation they ever had. Most people aren't drawn by the money, but by the idea. It's a challenge to see how they measure up competing against athletes masquerading around with names like Nitro, Thunder, Tower, Blaze, and Ice. Everyday heroes get their chance to take on larger-than-life heroes.

As the show takes off, suddenly there are photo shoots, press junkets, fan mail, appearances, all the usual sort of Hollywood-celebrity bullshit. We do *Good Morning America,* the *Tonight* show, *Live with Regis and Kathy Lee, Montel Williams, Sally Jesse Raphael, Extra, Geraldo, Entertainment Tonight, Talk Soup.* You name the press outlet, we are on it. That includes the cover of *TV Guide.*

I am no longer a bit player on the outside, my face pressed against the glass, looking in on a world I want to be a part of. I *am* the world. As the show explodes, I want to grow my body to keep up with the insatiable expectations, to be a larger-than-life figure, to be a hero.

I feel like I'm living the dream. I am proof that if a person works hard, and has endless tenacity, anything is possible. But beneath the layers of red, white, blue, and muscle is still the chubby kid who couldn't make weight in Pop Warner, who couldn't get his elementary-school classmate Monique Warner to kiss him, who denied being half-Asian because he was embarrassed.

I never feel special or privileged because of what has happened to me. Even more than in football, I know I can go from being a star one day to a nobody the next. My real fear is being forgotten.

The original version of *American Gladiators* is 100 hundred percent unscripted and there is *never* a predetermined outcome. Any contender can win any event at any time. They never spoon-feed us lines or give us suggestions on what to say or how to answer interview questions. We do everything on the fly, meaning that after an event they jam the microphones in our faces and ask us questions, because that's the way it's done in sports.

If I have a choice between being memorable or good, I'll pick memorable. Sure, stats last, but people really talk about the people who make an impression. They remember charisma and passion, and I make it my mission to be king of the interview. Nitro's popularity is no accident. It is a carefully orchestrated concerto. Each night I go home and study history, great battles, watch sports stories, read books . . . to come up with great lines I can use for the show. I always have an arsenal of one-line zingers ready. *If you're a minnow, you shouldn't swim with the sharks. It's always personal. If you didn't get hurt, you weren't trying hard enough. Either you love me or you hate me, but, if you hate me, you love to hate me.*

One of my favorite moments is when I dispatch an opponent in the contender ring, then bend down and kiss the auditorium floor. "This is my home," I roared. "And there ain't no man who is ever gonna throw me outta my home."

There are defining moments for my character . . . one comes from my battle with a contender named Lucian Anderson. In the heat of battle, I lose my pugil stick. Lucian keeps swinging at me, so I take him by the face and shove him off the platform. Let me be clear about this—I don't shove him because he beat me. That's not Nitro. I shove him because he keeps swinging. There's a difference. And his knowing that difference, I believe, is what makes Nitro so popular.

Gladiators is as real and in-your-face as it can get. That being said, certain contenders are a pain in the ass, and we may just give a little somethin' extra to beat this pain-in-the-ass contender and get him off the show. That's the general rule for contenders who are cocky. We make a concerted effort to sit them down and shut them up. We are big on respect. If a contender fails to bring his A game, then he gets no respect from me. Take a cheap shot and I'm going to drop you. I love to toe the line between rebel and lovable. I want to be the one the fans remember. I want be the one who the guys think is cool and the girls want to fuck.

That's why I'm the first Gladiator to be plasticized by Mattel. Mattel toys is spending millions of dollars developing a toy line for *American Gladiators* and wants me to consult on and promote the toy line.

When I show up at the Mattel headquarters, the rep takes me to the showroom floor where they have the toys spread across the table. When I first see my action figure, it's a huge letdown. He is only four inches tall.

"What's the deal?" I ask. "G.I. Joe is packing twelve and I'm only four inches? You're gonna give me an inferiority complex."

The rep tries to laugh it off. "Oh, come on. You're not serious."

"Yes, I am. G.I. Joe is twelve inches. That's how big the Gladiator doll should be. How heroic is four inches? Suppose you want G.I. Joe and the Nitro action figure to brawl. G.I. Joe is three times his size, is so whipping Nitro's ass, that's not cool."

"But the little green plastic army guys that have been around forever are only two inches tall," he responds, smiling like he's made a valid point.

I set him straight. "Yeah, but you get a whole bag of the little green guys. That's why they're called 'army guys' and don't have individual names. You lose one, who cares, you got fifty more. The Nitro doll is a single point-of-purchase item in its own packaging and should be packing twelve like G.I. Joe."

"Dan, it's done. There's nothing we can do."

He then unveils the rest of the toy line. He explains they have miniversions of the Atlasphere, the Wall, the Eliminator . . . and the action figures have to be smaller because they have to be able to integrate and play the games against a contender figure. I still think they're off base. Kids like action figures because they're fantasy-based, role-playing toys where they imagine they are the hero. They want to take their toys on impossible missions and crush and destroy everything they encounter. Four inches doesn't crush much.

At a toy fair at the plush Torrey Pines resort in San Diego, reps for toy sellers get their first look at Mattel's upcoming toy line. It's a ten-day event. I take my college roommate Bill with me for the first weekend. I do something that first night I've never done before. I take the drug ecstasy. Amped up on 'roids, and with my appetite for destruction, I can't just take one pill. I have to take five hits.

Bill and I end up tearing apart our suite at Torrey Pines. A security guard comes in the middle of the night after numerous complaints. We tell him to get the fuck out or we're going to kick his ass. He comes back later with a few more security guards. We tell them the same thing and shove the door closed in their faces. Then we continue to have a WWF match in the room, knocking over beds, throwing nightstands. I'm still surprised we didn't get arrested. And I'm still embarrassed about my despicable behavior.

The next day I sleep through the introductory breakfast meeting with Mattel. They hear about the raucous night before and, at lunch, threaten to fire me and send me home. I can't focus on what they are saying. I keep nodding my head and act like I'm listening. All the while, I'm telling myself to just get through the damn meeting. After what seems like an eternity, they feel I finally understand the importance of the event and lead me toward a set of double doors. I'm still buzzed, the room is spinning, but everything quickly settles when they open the doors, revealing thirty drop-dead gorgeous blondes, all dressed as Barbie.

There is work Barbie, housewife Barbie, *I Dream of Jeannie* Barbie, Malibu Barbie . . . I'm in heaven. I sample a few and end up with stay-at-home Barbie, a girl named Tiffany. As beautiful as she is cool, Tiffany is a NYC model, which gives her extra credibility in my eyes. She isn't some L.A. model/actress/stripper waitress. She's a New York model and she's my new girlfriend.

Barbie is a cultural icon. But no Barbie wants a Ken. Not for the fun, fuck-filled week. They want a bad boy. That's something I know how to be.

Thirty Barbies and Nitro in a plush resort for a week.

Thank you, Mattel.

Thank you.

———

After a great week at the toy fair, I come home and just feel like nothing. I wish I could say I'm angry or I hate myself, but the truth is, it's nothing that romantic or dramatic. I just feel like *nothing*. Nonexistent. I take my action figure, lie back on my bed, hold it up, and stare at it. The *American Gladiators* logo in red, white, and blue is pasted at the top of the package. A picture of me slamming a guy in Powerball is to the left of the logo. The figure itself is packed in a clear plastic bubble, so you can see it in full, huge muscles, glowering menace, and all.

I take the little four-inch plastic figure out of the package and run my fingers across the lines where they molded him together. He reminds me of Frankenstein. My mind drifts to an interview with Johnny Cash I read. He was asked what his favorite movie was. *Frankenstein,* he answered. He saw it when he was eight and never forgot the experience. When asked why, he grew quiet. Then he said, "Because the monster was stitched together out of these bad men, criminals who hurt people, and still he tried to be good."

This reminds me of my father.

It reminds me of myself.

At times I feel like a monster—a mad creation of science and technology, a scarred, damaged body built by terrible compounds, intent on doing evil, but with a heart that is kind and wants to do good. It's a head-splitting dichotomy. When I'm in the grip of my obsession with fame and steroids, I'm a monster. But I'm also trying to be a hero and role model for kids when role models are in short supply.

I'm trying to feed the beast of American consumerism. But I'm in over my head. I'm no match for the depths of my insatiable appetites, of my obsession. I don't realize that I'll never be big or strong enough to fill the dark spaces inside me. I don't know I'll almost die trying.

I flip on the radio, go into the bathroom, and place my action figure, my Frankenstein, on the bathroom counter. He stands there, all four inches, mocking me. He is taunting me with his appear-

ance. Even though he is only four inches, he is more muscular than I can ever be.

This is what they want. You'll never be me! You'll never be big enough or strong enough. You'll never be one of the beautiful people. You'll never be me!

I open the drawer and pull out a box of one-and-a-half-inch twenty-gauge syringes. The perfect weapon for my destruction. I strip off my clothes and stand naked in front of the mirror. I am puny in comparison to my action figure. I am only a man . . . he is a four-inch plastic god of contemptuous torment.

You'll never be me. You'll never be one of the beautiful people. You'll never be me!

He's right. I can never be like him, even though he was spawned from my image. But I do know how to grow bigger. "Spot injecting" is something I've heard about from a bodybuilder buddy. It's the practice of injecting directly into the muscle that you want to improve. My buddy said it is painful as hell but it works.

I look at my action figure and then back at myself. I line up syringes on the counter with the idea of injecting myself in each part of my body that is inferior to my little counterparts. They are *all* inferior.

I slam a syringe into the right flank of my chest like a shot of adrenaline. A jolt of pain streaks through my pec. I look into the mirror. Emptiness looks back at me. I let go of the syringe. It dangles from my chest.

Wham! I bury a syringe in my left pec. *The wounds that never heal can only be mourned alone.*

I plunge a syringe into my right thigh. *Anger like fire rages.*

My left thigh is punctured next. *The pain is obliterating. Shattering.* I'm not done. I need to hurt more.

I bang a syringe into each calf. *The beautiful people. The beautiful people.*

I jam a syringe into my left delt. *The anger. The need. Eating me alive.*

I slam a syringe into my right shoulder. *There is no excitement. There is no joy. There is only obsession.*

My eyes find the action figure's packaging. Oddly enough, on the box there's a warning: "CAUTION: Not Suitable for Children under 3. Contains small parts." It makes me start to think about all the kids who idolize me, and I'm filled with a rush of humanity. I try to lift the warm essence of my soul up out of my abused, pin-pricked container of a body . . . but then I hear myself emitting an ugly echoing laugh. At this moment, I realize that steroids and I are a match made in hell, and neither of us can get enough of each other.

CHAPTER 18

Road Warriors:
The 150-City
American Gladiators Tour

Like Alice in *The Adventures of Alice in Wonderland,* I've fallen into a hole and discovered a world I've never dreamed of. But I'm not dreaming this up. I'm living it. The Gladiators are going on a 150-city tour across America. That's right, clad in red, white, and blue, the Gladiators are coming to a city near you.

This tour is the brainchild of *American Gladiators* creator Johnny Ferraro, with an assist from concert promoter extraordinaire David Fishof. Johnny knows a thing or two about touring. Before creating *Gladiators,* he was a successful Elvis impersonator who played some of the world's largest venues. Fishof is coming off a successful Monkees reunion tour, and also Ringo Starr's tour.

I like Fishof the second I meet him. He's an Upper West Side New York Jew who understands the value and the wattage of star power. His goal is to quickly sign the two most popular Gladiators

167

and use them as the drawing linchpins of the tour. Everyone else can either join the team at a lower rate or stay home. He comes to Mike "Gemini" Horton and me first and makes us an offer we can't refuse. The other Gladiators sign on soon after, and the tour is born.

Ferraro and Fishof enlist Kenneth Feld, who owns and controls the Ringling Bros. and Barnum & Bailey Circus, to help set up the dates and secure the venues. The first big sponsor to come on board is 7-Eleven. They will help promote us in local markets by putting the Gladiators on Slurpee cups as well as by hosting special in-store ticket giveaways and chances to meet the Gladiators at the venue.

So let's add it all up. *Gladiators,* brought to you by an Elvis impersonator, a Monkees promoter, and the folks who brought you the circus. How could it be anything but the most insane Greatest Fucking Show on Earth?

Stay-at-Home Barbie is now my girlfriend. She's still living in New York, but she's been wanting to become Nitro's stay-at-home girlfriend. When I tell her about the ten-month tour, she volunteers to move to Los Angeles, stay at my place, and run the house while I'm gone.

I don't really know Tiffany well. I've never been in the same city with her for more than a week. But I do know she has a fondness for fruit. On one of her trips to California, Tiffany dresses in a tiny skirt, and when she bends over to grab something from the fridge, I'm thinking about how absolutely amazing her legs and ass look in her short skirt. I notice a banana in a bowl next to the fridge, and another thought springs to mind. I wonder how the banana would look inside her. I have a bad habit of saying whatever pops into my head.

"Hey, Tiffany, can I put this banana inside of you?"

She stands in the kitchen staring at me, her expression giving nothing away. I can't figure out if I'm in trouble or not. She lowers her chin and looks up at me with a mischievous naughty-schoolgirl grin and says, "Err . . . okay."

I walk over to the counter, pick up the banana, slide down her little white cotton panties, and slowly insert the banana. Foolishly, this is my litmus test, and Tiffany moves in. Luckily she turns out to be a great girl—the kind of person who has the windows washed, house cleaned, lawn mowed, checkbook balanced, and bills paid all before breakfast. She is much too together and organized, much too . . . like a wife.

That's the last thing I want. On the road I want to party like a rock star. We are rock stars with muscles. We thrive under the bright lights and screaming fans, we have groupies and sex, we have drugs, and we *can kick the shit out of you.* Our instruments are our pugil sticks, 100 mph tennis balls, and our fists.

Fishof tells us to pack light for the tour. There's only enough room on the tour bus for each of us to bring one large duffel bag of personal items. We're going to be in 150 cities in ten months, so the less we have to lug from city to city, from hotel to hotel, the better. I'm standing in my bedroom stuffing my belongings into an over-size duffel bag. Okay, I've got my spandex. Three pairs of sneakers. Two pairs of jeans. Some workout gear. A couple of dressy outfits for the nighttime. Socks, jocks, and—

Syringes.

Wait. Shit! How many syringes do I need for the road trip? Let me see . . . It's going to be a ten-month, 150-city tour. Ten months multiplied by four weeks equals forty weeks. Two shots a week equals . . . eighty syringes. Wait. No. I better make it ninety, just in case one breaks or the top comes off or whatever. Then it occurs to me. Where in the hell am I going to hide ninety syringes?

I bundle them together and sling an oversize rubber band around them and try to stuff them into a shoe. Not a chance. I divide them into two separate bundles of forty-five each. I wrap them both in rubber bands and try to cram then into a pair of shoes. They still won't fit. Hmmm. I divide the syringes into bundles of four, and they finally fit into two pairs of shoes. One big problem though. I'm only bringing three pairs of shoes and I barely have room for them.

I take a look at the calendar and realize we'll be coming back through California in three months. I exhale and reorganize my syringe supply accordingly. Absurd, right? Who else worries about the number of fucking syringes they have to pack? More people than you think. Nitro isn't alone.

In February 2007, Sly Stallone was arrested when he brought forty-eight ampoules of growth hormone through Australian customs while on his *Rambo* publicity tour. So Nitro and Rambo have something in common:

Syringes. Don't leave home without them.

With eighteen equipment-carrying semitrucks, three tour buses—one for the men, one for the woman, and one for the crew—and forty-five syringes (just counting mine), the Gladiators hit the road with the spirit of Elvis, the Monkees, and Ringling Bros. and Barnum & Bailey guiding our way. Johnny Ferraro brings a limo, hires a driver, and follows us, bringing up the rear.

The tour starts in New Orleans at the Superdome in front of twenty thousand screaming fans. The first time you play live, your heart explodes when twenty thousand individuals cheer your name. You never feel more alive. You're willing to rip the heart out of your own chest and hold it out to them, still pulsating in your hands, if that is what they demand.

Every night when we charge onto the arena floor, we want to give the audience the best show possible. We know people have so many ways to spend their entertainment dollars, and we are grateful, proud, and honored they choose to spend it on us. For Gladiators, it means laying it on the line each and every night. It means willingly throwing your body into the bone-crushing physical violence revered by the fans. It means there is *no way* our bodies can handle the punishment of doing a live show six nights a week, each night in a different city.

Thankfully, during the third week of the tour, the producers bring in a couple of "big bodies" to help with some of the heavy lifting on the tour, allowing the television Gladiators to pick their spots and moments to shine. For the big bodies, it's a bloody hard, endless barrage of thankless work. They have to parade around anonymously in our shadows, getting the shit beat out of them every night, with kids constantly stepping over, by, and around them to get our autographs, all for virtually no money. Lynn Williams is one big body who finds a way to hang on and impress throughout the tour and eventually earns himself a place on the television show, becoming Sabre. Victoria Gay (Jazz) and Lee Reherman (Hawk) are two others. They're all excellent additions to the show.

Everyone has his or her own aspirations for the tour. For some, it's a way to get paid or a chance to see America. For others, it's a chance to test their mettle against contenders from every state or to fuck a new conquest in every city.

For me, it's all of the above. It's a time to be reckless and crazy and celebrate the spoils of my hard-earned celebrity. I want to devour the essence of every city. I want to drink at the very fucking heart and feel the soul of our great country. This is before America is dying. This is when gas costs ninety cents a gallon, this is when Wesley Snipes pays taxes, and Sir Mix-a-Lot raps "Baby Got Back." These are great days, days like no others. Days when the median home price is $120,000 and you can get into the movies for four bucks and it means something to be an American.

These are days when American Gladiators are invading America.

And I thank God that Johnny Ferraro brings a limo, hires a driver, and follows us on tour because you can't take a tour bus to a nightclub. With Johnny, we paint the town. He's a big brother, a mentor, and a friend. He's first to catch us when we fall. And fall we do. So many nights we stumble into his limo, drunk out of our minds. He watches over all of us with a careful eye. I think it's in part because we are all like little brothers and sisters to him. And also because Gladiators were and are Johnny's baby and his life. Thanks to Johnny, not once in ten months of decadent indulgence do we get arrested or make the tabloids.

The tour becomes an endless barrage of cities all the same, but different. Faceless people, nameless girls. But never once do I forget a fan or a kid. I may abuse myself and my body, I may be broken. But when it comes to the *Gladiators* fans, it doesn't matter who the person is that wants my time—I'll stop and talk, even when I don't want to or I don't have the time. I hold the baby. I pose for the picture. I shake the little kid's hand and make him promise his parents he'll do well in school.

I'm this way because of an experience I had as a little kid in Minnesota. The star player of the Minnesota Vikings was scheduled to appear at the local grocery store as part of a promotion for the team. I waited with my brother, aunt, and uncle in the rain for hours, refusing to go home until I met my hero. He finally showed up two hours late and barely turned a glance at the mob of fans waiting for him. He signed a few autographs. The entire five minutes he was there, he acted as if it were a punishment. We were lucky he even showed up. Then he slipped back into his car and drove away. I didn't get an autograph that day.

I've never forgotten the slight. I promise myself never to be that guy. Why should I? I feel beautiful in the audience's eyes. I feel like a hero, like I'm breathing rarefied air. I feel loved. The sad thing is, I don't know how to get those feelings from those closest to me. I categorize my family members as brother, mother, sister, father, son. They are objects without emotions attached. I stand looking at them, waiting for a surprising new sensation to arise, and when it doesn't come, I'm disappointed and I curse myself for not knowing what I lack or how come I can't feel for them.

I would love for them to matter. I know they are supposed to.

———

Looking back, I know the loss of my brother obscured my vision and kept me at a distance from them. But back then, I fed with the fans under the glow of the stadium lights. I filled the empty places inside of me with the fans.

Still, the tour isn't all party and praise. About halfway through, the biggest conflict isn't with the contenders. It's from within as *Entertainment Tonight* and the *Enquirer* do a big exposé on Laser's significant other. Apparently she has a less-than-illustrious past. I don't need to rehash the details. The man's family has already suffered enough. The day the news splashes across the headlines, Jim is wrecked, absolutely destroyed. I remember his big, lumbering figure as he gets on the tour bus, his face etched in agony. The next thing I know, he's glaring at me and pointing his finger in my face.

"You fucker!" he screams.

I'm stunned. I have no idea why he's screaming at me. I feel the rage rise up in me. I scrapped with him a few years ago and I have no problem going at it with him again. Then it all comes out. Jim Kalafat thinks I'm the one who leaked the information to the media outlets. My rage quickly turns to sorrow. I feel sorry for the poor guy. Sorry that he's so screwed up by it he's actually accusing me— the very guy who helped get him on *Gladiators*. The very guy who let him stay in my family's home and eat off our dinner table for a few months between the Rams and moving to L.A. The guy who is supposed to be my best friend. I feel betrayed beyond belief by his delusions, and this is the end of our friendship.

With tempers and bad blood boiling, I'm happy to leave the road for a few weeks to work on a movie, *Death Becomes Her*, with Meryl Streep. That's right, I'm working with Meryl "I've Got a Gazillion Oscars" Streep.

You don't remember seeing me in it? You must've blinked. I'm only in it for a second, even though I spent three weeks working on it. My only line was cut. But for some reason (steroids make you stupid?) I think I'm going to be an integral part of the movie. I am about as important as a piece of furniture.

To add insult to injury, I take my seven-foot buddy, Olden Polynice, who is playing for the Los Angeles Clippers, to the premiere. When I first appear on the screen, a murmur goes through the crowd: "Hey, that's Nitro." When the scene finishes and I haven't said a line, Olden Polynice does the inconceivable.

In front of a packed audience that includes Meryl as well as other cast members, Bruce Willis and Goldie Hawn, Olden looks at me and yells, "Hey, man, aren't you going to say something?!" The entire theater erupts into laughter as I sink down in my seat, more embarrassed than I've ever been in my life.

After my big "acting" break I'm anxious to get back on the road—anxious to get back to being the main attraction. I rejoin the team in one of my favorite cities, Chicago. I have some great memories from the Windy City. I saw the legendary "Mike Ditka–fueled" Bears play the year they won the Super Bowl. I saw the unconquerable Jordan glide to one of his six NBA titles . . .

But when I see her, I know she'll be the memory of all memories from Chicago. Unfortunately, I'm not alone. I'm with a few of the other male Gladiators, backstage before the show, where this stunning brunette contender is stealing our hearts without even trying. I look over to Tower and say, "Amazing. I'm so all over that."

Tower looks at me and says, "I don't think so. She's mine."

I like a challenge, but it doesn't stop with the two of us. Viper, who is standing behind us, chimes in, "That's so not happening, fellas. I'm hooking up with her."

Oh, man, it's on—on like Donkey Kong. We start throwing out dollar amounts for a wager, each of us more confident than the next, when Ice walks up. "What're you guys doing?"

"We're making a little friendly wager on who is going to end up with that girl over there," I say, pointing her out.

Ice takes one look at her and says, "You guys are so stupid. That's just wrong. You shouldn't be betting on who's going to hook up with a girl."

"Oh, you're just jealous," barks Viper.

Ice just rolls her eyes, shakes her head, and walks off.

The three of us wait until after the show to make our move. We wade through the crowd backstage and set up camp outside the contender's dressing room in anticipation of her exiting. We wait for the longest time, then finally we ask a woman to go into the locker room in search of the mysterious brunette. A few moments later she comes out and tells us the room is empty. We are all stunned. How in the hell did she get by us?

That's when we hear Ice call out, "Hey, boys!"

We snap our heads around to find Ice across the backstage floor with a shit-eating grin on her face, hand in hand with the stunning brunette. "Have a good night!" she hollers, and leaves with the brunette, taking home the biggest prize of the night.

After ten months, the tour has become an endless string of performances, different cities, and different hotels. Our bodies are beat. We're tired of sleeping in a new hotel every night and living out of a suitcase. Even though this is what we live for, bleed for, work so hard for, each show begins to feel like a chore. It gets harder and harder to rise to the occasion and face the local heroes who are so intent on getting their piece of fame and proving their athletic prowess. We have nothing left to give and are looking forward to going home.

A friend meets up with me in Tennessee and brings me a couple of vials of my running mate from Italy, Parabolin, to get me over the hump. Since my first tangle with this drug, I know it to be toxic and intoxicating. I know I have to be careful, but I also want to be ready for the biggest stop on the tour: Madison Square Garden.

As our bus pulls up to our hotel in Manhattan, I close my eyes and lean my head against the back of the seat, waiting to see if I can conjure up the feeling I have every time I step onto the arena floor. A tingling sensation shoots down my spine like lightning splitting a tree. I open my eyes, smiling, reassured, and excited. I know I can rise above the drop-dead exhaustion and bring it tonight in the Garden with a barbaric savagery that will be breathtaking.

But I also notice another feeling. A feeling that something isn't quite right. It's an unsettling nuisance of a feeling that has been knocking on the door of my subconscious. It's not unhappiness. Day in and day out, I persevere despite knowing that I have never been 100 percent happy. But this other feeling has been with me since San Jose, and no matter how many people are in the auditorium cheering their hearts out, a part of me is somehow still deadened to the roar, immune to it, unable to feel it. Nothing is ever enough.

We check into the hotel, and when I go up to my room, a FedEx envelope is waiting for me on the table. I open it and take out the documents. It's the initial rough sketches for the nonprofit charity I'm starting up. I place them on the table and stare at them.

NITRO'S KNIGHTS: GLADIATORS AGAINST DRUGS.

All at once, it hits me . . . I'm a liar. I'm a fucking liar. I can't go out and spearhead this charity that tours schools, speaking to kids about not using drugs. My heart won't let me do it. Something decent is still inside me that hates what I'm doing and how dirty it feels. I'm taking these drugs that inspire the admiration and worship of kids, and in the next breath I'm standing in the pulpit, preaching to kids not to take drugs. Sure, I can rationalize that I'm older and I know what I'm doing, and they're young and impressionable, but that's all bullshit. Yet still, I don't quit. I keep drinking the Kool-Aid and playing the game.

At the same time, I'm furious with myself for the momentary lapse in what I perceive as my wall of strength—for allowing this intrusion of emotion to seep through the fortress of my being. Now, I want and need to punish someone. I need to feed.

I carry the rage, this anger like fire, with me when I burst onto the arena floor of Madison Square Garden in front of fifteen thousand cheering fans slamming to their feet. I get lost in the reverberations, the chaos, the chants.

Nitro. Nitro. Nitro.

When I blast into my opponent, the world slips away, and for a moment the voices are quiet. For one moment the world is in sweet and simple order and I feel myself rising to the heavens, igniting and blowing up any dark, hidden places within.

I exit the arena while they cheer. I head into the locker room, where I sit, my head slumped, my body still shooting adrenaline. I lock myself in an empty stall, and there, all alone, I sit on the toilet in the shadows. I feel something warm and stinging on my face. I touch the bud of moisture on my cheek and realize it's a tear.

I am crying.

I am fucking crying.

The concept is so foreign to me, it's like I'm a deaf-mute, suddenly able to speak. I am completely overwhelmed and shattered. I feel shame . . . weakness . . . and fragility. My mind blasts to the last time I cried. It was twelve years ago in the hospital, in a drug-induced stupor, after knee surgery. I feel the waves roll deep within me. I feel vulnerable. I feel lost. I hurdle back further in time. I'm ten years old, on my knees, weeping in front of my brother Randy's inert body, which lies on a slab of steel in the morgue. I feel alone. The gates are opening. I feel a profound sense of loss. I'm four years old standing on a plane sobbing, as I see my mother and sister disappearing out of my life through the closing door of an airplane. I'm told, "Big boys don't cry." I am alone in the frigid solitude of my plight.

I reach down and touch my chest. I can feel my hurt pounding inside me. I haven't felt these feelings in so long. I have not felt these feelings since *he died.*

I have entered a new world. I've entered the world of *feeling*.

I hear the whoops and hollers of the other Gladiators as they enter the locker room, the crowd still shrieking in the background. I wipe my tear-dampened cheeks, rise to my feet, and reach for the handle of the stall, but I don't open it. I cannot stop my tears. I slump back on the toilet and remain there silently sobbing.

CHAPTER 19

Liar, Liar

In Los Angeles, on this night, I know I am having a breakdown. I am making more money than I ever have in my life. I am famous. I am on TV. I am standing in my bathroom looking in the mirror, my heart pounding like a jackhammer. I am blinking rapidly. I am deeply conflicted and confused. I am reaching for a bottle of Vicodin, my best friend since the start of season two and a bone-crushing collision on Powerball. I am choking back the last two soul-stealers. I am swallowing them dry.

I am trying to swallow the news.

Lyle Alzado is dead.

Lyle Alzado, the Brooklyn-born former lineman whose fierce play for the Los Angeles Raiders made him the apotheosis of ferocity and who later became a self-styled symbol of the dangers of steroid abuse, died yesterday at his home in Portland, Oregon. He was 43 years old.

—*The New York Times*

Forty-three. Forty fucking three. Just a few years ago, I was sitting with Lyle at his restaurant when he was at the top of his game. Yesterday death seemed like a lifetime away. Today it's here. The stark reality is staring me square in the face.

I walk into my bedroom and open my nightstand drawer. A magazine is buried underneath everything else—hidden—as a way not to deal. I sit on the bed, the sweet serenity of the Vicodin beginning to wash over me. I hold the *Sports Illustrated* in my hand. I have to deal now.

Alzado is on the cover. He looks so fragile and full of fear. Just a shadow of what he once was, the most feared man in football. The headline splashed across the top of the article reads:

"I'm Sorry . . . I Lied."

He's a liar. He's a fucking liar! I'm a liar. I'm a fucking liar! I'm fucked. He's fucked-up. He's dying. He's dead. I'm dying inside. I inhale, taking in as much air as I can, to calm myself. The emotions well up in me. I am feeling again. I feel weak and pathetic. I want to cry. I hate feeling. I hate not being in control. I hate being at the mercy of these . . . feelings. I breathe again. I know the air will calm my thoughts.

I feel something pushing its way forward. Vomit. I rush to bathroom and vomit into the toilet. My heart is racing and there are . . . feelings. Feelings struggling to the surface. I fight them. I reach to flush the vomit away, to flush my feelings away, and I see the Vicodin. I remember they are my last two. I reach into the soup. There is vomit and Vicodin in my hand.

I clench my fist around the little white pills and I squeeze until the vomit slithers between my fingers and my hand is white and trembling. I am trembling with shame, anger and—RAGE.

This is the feeling I've been trying to summon up. This is where I feel at home. This is where I live. I rise to my feet filled with the rage and fury. I flip on the bathroom faucet and bend down to drink. I swallow the Vics back down and stare in the mirror and load up a shot of testosterone and plunge it into my ass in defiance. In defiance of weakness . . . life . . . death.

I head downstairs, grab a bottle of vodka, and take a big swig to wash down anything remaining. But emotions still stab through me. I'm feeling . . . sadness . . . loss . . . Not for Alzado, but for someone else. For *him. My brother.*

The house suddenly seems claustrophobic, the very walls are squeezing my lungs, compressing, making it a struggle to breathe.

I need to stop feeling. I need to fuck or fight.

I get in the car and drive down Ventura Boulevard. The city flashes by me in a blaze of neon. I take a turn toward Van Nuys and go deep into the violent heart of the city. There is a strip bar here. I chug back more vodka. The buzz of Vicodin and alcohol is strong. I think about a stripper at the club I'm friendly with. I turn into the Warehouse District as images dance in my head of the last time we hooked up. She likes it hard. And dirty. Just what I need.

A car cuts me off. I slam my fist on the horn. Speed after the car. The car screeches to a stop in front of me. Three guys get out and walk toward my car.

I'm not going to fuck. I am going to fight.

I exit my car. They are tattooed, wearing wifebeaters and bandannas. They look like something out of a bad late-night cable movie. They're coming toward me, their chests puffed out, full of youth and stupidity. They are puny and will get crushed.

"Hey, ese . . . you gotta problem?" one guys says.

The second guy bounces toward me, gesticulating with his hands. "What the fuck you thinking, cutting us off?"

If he takes one more step toward me, he's going to be taking a nap. He wisely doesn't get any closer.

"I got no problem," I say.

"Get the fuck back in the car or we gonna fuck you up!" he hollers.

He takes my lack of aggression as a weakness. I am drunk. I stumble.

"Yeah, get the fuck back in the car before you get fucked up, you fuckin' drunk!" another one barks.

They should see that I'm not scared. I am willing.

"Let's do this," I say, motioning them toward me.

I feel sorry for them. Because I know I'm not going to stop until I hurt them.

"Let's fucking do this!" I scream.

They glance furtively to each other. They are afraid. They thought there was strength in numbers. They thought they were going to jump out of the car and intimidate me.

"Come on, let's fuck him up," one of them says, a nervous quaver in his voice. No one moves. They don't want this.

I *need* this.

I yell at them, "Come on, you fucking little pussies! What the fuck is wrong with you! I thought you wanted a piece of me!"

No one moves. They're intimidated by my size. They can sense I want this. They're looking for a way out. They start saying things like "Get outta here, ya drunk." "We're gonna let you off this time, man."

They think it's over. It's not. I spit on one of them.

I'm wrong. I'm sick. I need help.

I am fighting.

The first guy rushes in. I drop him with an overhand right. The second guy swings wildly at my head. I duck, reposition my weight and slam a thundering left hook into his ribs. He screams like a little bitch. He screams the way Max Schmeling did when Joe Louis pummeled him in the ribs in their rematch.

I don't see the third guy. I *feel* him jump on my back and start to choke me. He's heavier and stronger than I expect. I can't get him off me. Someone grabs my leg. I'm kicking him. Stomping him. Crushing him. He won't let go. They won't let go.

Suddenly my brain explodes in a blast of pain. I've been hit by something. I fall to the ground. I see a lead pipe flash into view. It connects again. Screaming-white pain blasts through me, obliterating my senses. I see and feel feet and fists punching and kicking me.

I roll over onto all fours and cover my head with my arms, trying to protect myself. The blows continue to rain down and punish me. I'm losing. I'm getting beaten. They won't fucking stop. I grab the foot of the pipe holder and rip him to the ground. I have a handful of his hair and start slamming his head into the concrete. He's the screamer. He screams. And screams.

His friends are kicking me. I won't stop. His friends are suddenly screaming. Everyone is screaming at me to stop. I hear them. I don't hear them. I hear them. I stop and roll off. They rush in and attend to their friend. I stagger to my feet, bloody and bruised. I stand. I'm wobbly. I don't feel the pain yet. But I know it will come.

There are sirens. I know the cops will be here shortly. We're gone in an instant, the only evidence of us is blood. Their blood. My blood.

I race away in the car. I can taste the blood in my mouth. I slide my tongue over my teeth, happy they're all there. I hurt now. There is pain everywhere. I drink more vodka. I look in the rearview mirror. My face looks like something you'd find in the meat section at the grocery store. Blood is everywhere. I suddenly feel the need to get higher. I reach into the center console, pull out a small Scope bottle half-filled with the drug GHB. I drink it all. I know it's too much. But I think it's a good cocktail to oblivion: vodka, Vicodin, testosterone, blood, and too much GHB. I know I shouldn't drive.

I pull into my driveway and hobble unsteadily into the house, a sense of dread overwhelming me, accompanied by a visceral queasiness. I head upstairs to the bathroom. And I feel it again. The very thing I am trying to avoid. The very thing I've *always* tried to avoid. The feelings of life . . . the past. They keep swelling inside me. Haunting me. They are relentless. They are my tormentor. They've pierced through the sheaths of muscle, and found their way into my brightest days. I can't escape them. They are like the air I breathe.

Time has tapped me on the shoulder.

I bury my face in my hands, tormented by the thousand lacerating emotions. Then suddenly, everything is welling up inside me.

I vomit forcefully into the toilet again. I remain there, shaking, choking.

I am crying.

The tears come in little waves until they're a deep, wrenching sob. The sobs of loss. The sobs of wounds that will never heal. I gasp for breath. My chest moves up and down rapidly. I am whimpering. I am sniveling. I am breathing. I am feeling. I am living. I am high. I am so fucking high.

One feeling rises above the rest: the urge to vomit again. I heave into the toilet over and over. It's as if my innards are ripping free from my insides and just trying to get out. I puke harder, more violently. I cannot stop. I'm trying to puke up the past. To put it out into the world in all of its nakedness.

When I finally stop vomiting, I long to feel the comfort of my bed. I pull myself to my feet and hang on to the sink for balance. I look at myself in the mirror. Blood is caked on my face, scrapes and bruises are littered across my torso and arms. I turn the faucet on and splash water on my face. I stand. I am unsteady. I look back in the mirror and see someone standing next to me, and it scares the shit out of me.

But in an instant I know him.

It's my brother. He's weeping.

I'm weeping. I reach out to touch him. He disappears into the ether. I miss him. I miss him so fucking much.

I know I'm hallucinating.

I stumble to my bed, pass out, and dream.

I'm seeing my son being born. I'm reexperiencing his birth. The birth of my son isn't just music. It's the most profound, heartfelt music ever created. My throat knots as I see his head crown, and it only gets worse from there. As the tiny astonishment of life pushes forward, I have to sit because I'm trembling so badly. I can only watch, thunderstruck, as the staggering brilliance of the experience washes over me. It's vast, it's relentless, it's unfair—this happening, which moves even the most hardened human soul, transforming me into a defenseless man.

Tears flow unchecked down my face as I realize, all at once, what we are: life . . . and love and death. I am helpless in their spell. I feel the blackness of sleep coming. I hold on, trying to savor every morsel of the experience. There is nothing but blackness.

When the dim rays of the morning sun filter through the blinds, I awaken and step out onto the balcony. I stare out at the great red rim of the sun as it rises over the mountains. I gaze, mesmerized by it, as though I've never seen it before. I hurt. A new kind of hurt. Something more than the brain-numbing hangover, more than the excruciating, splitting pains of battle. I hurt with the desire to remember. Fresh tears streak down my cheeks. For the first time in my life, I *choose* to remember. I *choose* to welcome the memories— and that makes all the difference.

I remember the funeral procession and the parade of flowers down Cach Mang Street in Saigon. I remember my dad crying so fucking hard I thought he was going to bleed tears. I remember not crying. I remember the moth on Randy's coffin and the elation of the Buddhist monks, believing this was my brother reincarnated. I remember his gentle smile. I remember throwing the first handful of dirt on his grave. I remember his protective embrace. I remember the days following his death when it did nothing but rain and the Vietnamese monks told me it was "Buddha rain," the rain that would cleanse our karma from the war. To me, it meant that God cried for all of the people that died in the war. He cried for all of his children . . . including my brother. Including me.

I remember Randy.

I remember that I never got a chance to say good-bye.

I'm weeping openly now, on the balcony, in the naked light of the morning sun. I'm filled with the crushing desire to live. But I don't know how. I'm filled with the desire to stop steroids. But I don't know how. I'm filled with the desire to be a better man. But I don't fucking know how.

I only know that something is wrong. And I'm tired.

Tired like I've never been before.

Tired of living the lie.

CHAPTER 20

The Biggest Mistake

In the hush of night, the four most popular Gladiators call a clandestine meeting. Zap, Gemini, Ice, and I huddle together in a trailer at the eleventh hour. In two days, season four is scheduled to begin, and there's a big problem—it's staring me in the face as I look at the list of merchandising licenses that Samuel Goldwyn Company holds for the *American Gladiators*. I scour it. The over seventy-five items include a Nintendo video game, a Mattel toy line complete with action figures, T-shirts, sweaters, hats, jackets, trading cards, posters, a complete vitamin line, Halloween costumes, lunch pails, 7-Eleven Slurpee cups, toothpaste, workout water bottles, and protein bars.

The estimated revenue for these products is in the hundreds of millions—a testament to the success of the show. This is fantastic for the Samuel Goldwyn Company. And it's great for the Gladiators— except for one huge problem:

WE AREN'T GETTING A PIECE!

That's right. It's our pictures, our bodies, our faces, on all the merchandise offerings. It's our blood, our sweat, and our broken

188 / Dan Clark

bones strewn across the arena floors, but—it's all their money.

Our reps have been reaching out to the producers for months to discuss the problem, but they get no reply. After all, in our initial contracts, we signed away our rights. We were young and stupid and looking to make a quick buck. Who knew the show was going to become a smash hit? Being a Gladiator is a dream job for most of us. For the first three years, living the dream was enough to carry us through the battles and hard times. We did it for more than the money. It was important to us. Now, in the fourth year, we're all running on empty and we want to get paid. We are having the clandestine meeting as a result of our naïveté, and the Samuel Goldwyn Company's unwillingness to share.

The physical cost on our bodies is skyrocketing. Injured and breaking down, we are running out of real estate—there is only so much of our bodies left that isn't destroyed.

Big Mike, aka Gemini, the patriarch of the group, speaks first. "If they don't give us a piece, I'm not going to show up for work."

I nod in agreement. So does Raye.

Lori, aka Ice, says, "Screw them."

"We just want what's fair," I reiterate.

"Yeah, we're not trying to break new ground. Just give us the industry standard," Mike continues.

"Do you think we could lose our jobs over this?" Ice asks.

"There's no possible way," our rep says. "Your faces are on all the toys, video games, and products. It'd be death for them, and there'd be a lot of questions to answer with the merchandisers, especially Mattel. Mattel has spent millions of dollars on the toy line, and to have the core characters absent from the show would be a nightmare."

Mike looks at the group and says, "We all have to stick together on this no matter what happens. That's where our strength is." He pauses for a moment to let it sink in. "All right, so we agree that's the plan, right?"

We all answer strongly. But, in Raye's eyes, I catch a glimmer of uncertainty. I make a mental note of it. When we all get up to leave, I tell our rep, "I just want to make sure you're clear that we're only asking for what's fair—the industry standard for merchandising on TV shows." He nods that he gets it.

The next day our rep calls the Samuel Goldwyn Company to schedule a meeting. They aren't interested until he tells them if they don't have the meeting to hear our requests, we aren't showing up on the set the following day.

On the day of the big meeting Big Mike and I have lunch together while we wait to hear from our rep about the outcome of the meeting. We hate the idea of holding the show hostage, but it's the only way to get the Samuel Goldwyn Company to come to the negotiating table. And we're both confident that the deal will get done. We're only asking for what's fair, and we believe, in our hearts, that we deserve it. After all, underneath the glamour of the red, white, and blue, *American Gladiators* is a vicious, full-contact sport that decimates souls and leaves body parts strewn across the floor.

Imagine having to have nine surgeries, including seven shoulder operations (complete tears of rotator cuffs, labrum tears), lower-back surgery for a slipped disk, fracture of zygomatic bone (under eye), a broken nose, three broken fingers, radial-nerve damage to the right forearm, a broken right toe, and a slipped disk in the neck.

If that doesn't make you appreciate the way we kill ourselves for our sport, the fact that the above surgeries were for one Gladiator, alone, should set you straight. That list wasn't mine, but we all had our lists. The risk level of Gladiators is much higher than in professional football, and in a stratosphere by itself. And because we are putting our bodies on the line nightly, we feel it is mandatory to get a piece of the merchandising to protect us in case we wind up with a career-ending injury. It seems unfathomable, practically impossible, that this will end with anything but a good deal for us.

Big Mike's phone rings. It's our rep. The news isn't good. He tells us that Samuel Goldwyn himself said, "My father didn't renegotiate, I don't renegotiate. They either come to work tomorrow or they're fired."

I'm stunned. Completely floored. But I believe it's part of the negotiation.

I look to see how Big Mike is taking it. "Fuck it!" he says. "I'm not going back."

I don't have the same fire of conviction. Mike has a wife and two young sons. He has anchors. His life stretches beyond the spandex. Yes, I have a son. My son is my "little buddy" who comes up on weekends. We hang out and then I send him back home to his mother. I still don't know how to embrace the magnificence of the gift of fatherhood. I have so much of my identity wrapped up in being a Gladiator. I'm filled with the threat of losing something I love deeply.

But I agree with Big Mike. I can't go back. It's about pride, integrity, and a value of self. It is rightful indignation. And in truth, another part of me still believes this is just tactics, that Samuel Goldwyn is going to come back with a better offer. I believe he will be fair. He has to be. It's the right thing to do.

I'm wrong. Dead wrong. There is no offer besides "Show up or get fired."

I'm young, naive, and out of a job. I'm livid, hurt, and I feel betrayed.

As the weeks pass, those emotions begin to fade and I can think clearly. The apocalyptic signs were there from day one. It is now crystal clear that one of Samuel Goldwyn's fears was that the Gladiators would become stars. Why was that a fear? Because stars get—

PAID.

His tightfisted way of thinking serves him well in the independent moviemaking world, where story is king. Samuel Goldwyn is quoted as saying, "Stories make stars, not vice versa."

But this isn't a highbrow independent movie like *The Madness of King George* or *Eat Drink Man Woman*. Gladiators are a different kind of animal. We are a groundbreaking, high-octane, in-your-face, bombastic, trash-talking sports-competition show. And *stars* are exactly what drives the show.

It's insane to me that Samuel Goldwyn doesn't get it.

But I believe there's another reason Samuel Goldwyn says no. He doesn't want *American Gladiators* to be his legacy. He comes from a legendary Hollywood family and is considered Hollywood royalty. His dad, Samuel Goldwyn Senior, was one of Hollywood's pioneer moguls, the G in MGM. Little Sam Goldwyn, living in the shadow of his legendary father, doesn't want to be remembered as the G in *American Gladiators*. Sam wants to be in the glamorous business of making movies just like his father, and to fund this passion he bleeds his enduring cash cow, *American Gladiators*, dry.

Eventually, Goldwyn will fall victim to his own grand ambitions. The company will plow $11 million—a fortune at that time in the world of independent filmmaking—into *The Perez Family,* a poorly received comedy starring Marisa Tomei and Anjelica Huston that grosses only $2.5 million domestically. Eleven million into a risky, unknown venture. Zero more into a known commodity like *American Gladiators*. A few years later, the company will be on the chopping block and in $60 million of debt. But that comes later.

After we walk away from the show, Raye goes begging for her job back. I don't think it weakens our position. I think it's done and over. Even though she goes back on her word to the others in the group, I don't hold it against her. All have to do what they have to do for themselves.

In the next several months, I see that pigs get fat and then they get slaughtered. The Samuel Goldwyn Company continues to trot out muscle-heads dressed in the red, white, and blue with names like Bronco, Flame, and Cyclone. But these guys aren't the real thing. Their faces are not on the merchandising. They aren't Gladiators and they don't fool the audience for one minute. The ratings take a big hit.

I watch all of this from afar. I'm tired and I need time off. Once again I have no idea what to do with my life but rest and heal. The toll the steroids have taken on my body has never been more apparent. Everything hurts. The wind blows and it hurts. I feel like I just want to disappear for a while.

I jump off the juice. The inevitable, dreaded crash soon follows. It isn't like a punch in the gut. It's more like a hot-air balloon with a slow leak. The air keeps seeping out until you're flat on the ground, unable to fly.

I spend a lot of time with a chiropractor, James Pressley, and at a place called the Soft Tissue Center, where they try to put my body back together after years of abuse. I spend thousands on the top acupuncturist in Los Angeles. I chug bottles of anti-inflammatories. I feel the desire to come clean. I am feeling all the pain of the years of abusing my body. I'm not pissing blood. I'm not having a heart attack. I'm simply in a lot of pain. There is no way I'm going back to *Gladiators*.

Seeing the ratings decline is bittersweet. It feels good to be right, to know that we, the most popular Gladiators, were the heart of the show. Each week, as the ratings erode, the satisfaction of being right diminishes, until I feel like I'm watching something I love die slowly in front of me.

I get a call from them. They ask if I'd consider coming back. But they still can't get Sam to budge on the merchandising issue. I flat out refuse, even though I miss it so much. I miss the cheers of the audience. I miss having a place to belong. I miss the hits and violence. I miss that sweet and simple place where the world makes sense. You see, *Gladiators* is something I was able to do better than anyone else in the world. I was the Tiger Woods, Michael Jordan, Alex Rodriguez, of red, white, and blue spandex. So no matter how insignificant it may be in the grand scheme of life, it is *really something* to be the best at a particular thing in life. How many people can say that?

A few weeks later, *Gladiators* calls again. They sweeten the deal. If I come back as Nitro for one season, they dangle the carrot that I can host the following season. Hosting is something I always aspired to do. But still I say no. If I return without a piece of the merchandising, walking away will have meant nothing. My resolve is strong. Without a piece of the merchandising, it'll be a cold day in hell before I return.

In the afternoon, I go to a charity event for the Children's Hospital in Los Angeles. I'm in a room with a group of ten to twelve sick kids who are all big *Gladiators* fans. For many of them, their life span isn't counted in years. It's counted in weeks, days . . . hours. To see their unbridled joy, their smiles in spite of their death sentences, breaks my heart. One little six-year-old boy is so weak and sick, it seems it hurts him to open his eyes. The staff tells me he doesn't talk much. He's suffering through a harsh bout of chemo to kill the cancer in his brain. The nurse lets me know he's the biggest *Gladiators* fan of all.

I kneel beside his bed. His entire face lights up. "Nitro," he whispers in a raspy, dry voice.

"Hey, what's up, little man?" I beam at him.

He manages to squeak out, "You're my favorite Gladiator. I wish you were . . . on the show." Merely speaking hurts him, causing him to use a tremendous amount of the little energy he has left. I feel a lump in my heart the size of a glacier as he strains to continue, "When you run . . . I run. When you jump . . . I jump. When you win . . . I win." He smiles, then closes his eyes. I stand there thunderstruck. It has taken everything his little body has to communicate those words to me.

He dies a few weeks later.

The pleas of a young kid can soften the hardest soul. But I know the road to any comeback has to go through the medicine cabinet. I strap up the proverbial chin strap and go to my bathroom and pull out an array of steroids. I don't want to take a lot, just enough to get me over the hump. Just enough to allow me to compete. The more I listen to my internal dialogue, the more I realize I sound like a junkie. I have my needles. I have my kit. I have my secret.

I remove the vial marked Deca-Durabolin. I raise the small amber vial to the bulb of the bathroom light and stare at its golden-ness. Long and deep. Lost in it. I load up a syringe, slam it into my glute, but it bounces off. The needle will not pierce the skin. Once, this drug made me feel so invincible . . . now it makes me feel like a phony. Abruptly, I put it back in the drawer, turn off the light, exit the bathroom, and go to bed.

I stare up at the ceiling and tell myself I'm going to make my comeback naturally—steroid-free. I exhale deeply, comforted by the thought. Yes, I'm going to do this naturally. I close my eyes to sleep. Can't. I'm blinking, staring at the wall. I'm besieged by the insidious voice of expectations and not being strong enough. I want to walk into the bathroom and slam a syringe into my ass, then pull it out and slam it in again. Over and over. I want the voices to stop.

I flip the covers off, get up, and head for the bathroom. I stand in the threshold of the door for a long moment, tormented. Then, I turn and abruptly leave the room. I need some distance from the drugs, I need something to clear my mind. I go to the next bed-room. My son is here for the weekend. He's sleeping in the bed. He's been with me more since the dream.

I crawl in and slide next to him. His body is warm. I put my hand on his chest and feel the beat of his little heart against my cal-loused palm. I realize this is the first time I've taken a moment to feel his heartbeat. The rhythm is steady and strong. It flutters against my hand. I'm amazed by the miracle of life. He doesn't wake and I count the beats of his heart as a way to quiet the voices. My last thought is *Yes, I can do this*. Then I fall into a deep, dream-less sleep.

The next morning I awaken with a start, heart pounding, face slickened with sweat, like an addict going through withdrawal. I burst back into the bathroom and fumble through the cabinet with shaking hands. I snatch out the Deca, load it into a syringe as quickly as my trembling fingers can manage, and thrust it into my glute. As I depress the plunger and start to release the soothing oil into my body—

"Dad . . . ?"

I turn, stunned to see my sleepy-eyed five-year-old son framed in the doorway. I stare at him, caught completely off guard, at a loss for words. Finally I get out, "Go back . . . go back to bed . . ."

He can't take his eyes off the syringe in my ass.

"Go back to bed," I say with more force.

Still he doesn't move. Tears brimming in his little eyes, he opens his mouth to speak. His voice quivers. "Is Daddy . . . is Daddy . . . sick?"

An unendurable assault of emotion surges through me. Shame. Revulsion. I put a shadow of a smile on as my insides twist. "Yes . . . daddy's sick. Go back to bed, so he can take his medicine."

I am sick. I need help.

Tyler takes in a stiff breath to fight off the tears, then turns around and walks out.

I catch sight of myself in the mirror. Haggard. Tired. Ashamed.

I feel a deep pit inside me. Pain stabs through my glute from the needle's prolonged intrusion into my body. I return my attention to it. I hesitate another instant, feeling my insides turn. Then I regurgitate the rote dogma that has been the boilerplate of my entire existence. *I need to do this. It's the only way I can compete. The only way I am someone.* I'm deeply conflicted—twisting, nearly breaking inside, but ultimately I feel I have no choice but to depress the plunger.

I close my eyes a moment, trying to still my aching heart. I think about the things I saw with my father . . . the heart attack, the hookers, the spousal abuse, and the drugs, and still I love him.

I hope, after this, my son will still love me.

I hope . . . he will forget.

———

In the end, when the unimaginable blinks on the scoreboard, when the unthinkable dances on the arena floor, the cheers drown out the *American Gladiators* theme song.

All but one word.

"Nitro! Nitro! Nitro!"

Around the arena, every heart is pounding, every chest rising with raw emotion. *Gladiators* fans, giddy, chant my victory song, "Wild thing! You make my heart sing!" I charge out onto the arena floor. The spotlight hits me. I stand stock-still, then thrust a fist up in the air like a revolutionary black Olympic sprinter. The house explodes with cheers.

I'm back on the show not only to get paid, I'm here to kick ass and fulfill my promise to the audience, to use my body to destroy all those in my path, to entertain. But from the first collision, I realize something has been stolen from me. It's just one event, just one hit, just the beginning. But it feels like a lifetime.

An *ending*.

The fire has always burned fiercely within me, to beat, crush, and destroy any and every opponent standing in front of me. I have never cared if they're bigger, faster, or stronger. I have always been hell-bent on winning—at any cost. But now, I'm an aging champion, throwing my last punches. Now, the bone-crushing hits don't bring the same satisfaction.

Now, the fire is dying.

I spend the first half of season five trying to rekindle the flame. The time off, the battles, the years of steroid abuse, have taken something out of me that will never come back. Getting ready for each show becomes a bigger chore. Everything is harder. I feel deep inside that something is moving out of my grasp. After battling over five hundred contenders on the tour and on the live show, I decide to stop fooling myself and finally accept it.

The fire is out.

I no longer feel the need to be a beast, to try to destroy. Those dark places are still dark, but they're different. I don't feel the need to crush. I feel the need to understand the light struggling to shine through the dusty window of my soul.

I limp through the rest of the season, always grateful, always thankful for the audience support. But the desire to get off steroids, to stop putting the poison into my body, grows stronger and stronger until it's all I can think about. I count the days for production to finish. On the last day, I smile more than I have in a long time.

As I finish the last event, I drink in the adoration like a vampire. I lap up every cheer, every hoot, every hand raised in victory, trying to make the wonderful moment last forever. Because I know it's the end. Not just to Nitro, but to a mind-set, a lifestyle, an entire way of being. I have nothing left to give. Yes, I'm leaving behind something I love so dearly, but I'm comforted that I'm walking toward a new life.

CHAPTER 21

Nitro Must Die!

The only way I can beat the steroid addiction is to kill Nitro. The cocky, in-your-face, aggressive competitor has to die, for Dan Clark to live.

One big problem. Nitro is a tough son of a bitch and isn't easy to kill.

After more than half a decade of playing him, somewhere along the line I've lost sight of myself. I no longer know where Nitro stops and I begin. The traits that make him a helluva of a Gladiator also make him a monster to kill.

The first few weeks of being clean are easy. I run around feeling fantastic, shrugging off the pitfalls of the steroid crash, emboldened by the new direction of my life. For the first time in fourteen years, I truly feel steroid-free. I feel I have the strength and conviction to keep clean. I know I'm sitting on the edge of a new life. It's right in front of me in the form of a microphone. It's the seventh year of *Gladiators*. I'm set to cohost with Mike Adamle. I'll be wearing a sport coat. There is absolutely no need for me to take steroids.

It's been six weeks since I punctured my flesh with a needle or swallowed a steroid. I get dressed. My shirt hangs loosely off my body. It's an odd feeling. I'm so used to my impossibly thick chest and arms testing the seams of my shirts. I'm so used to the tight fit that accentuates every contour. I feel the urge, the powerful pull of steroids. I put on the tightest workout shirt I can find. I want it to strangle my body, cut off the blood to my brain. To kill the urge. To kill the compulsion. To kill Nitro.

I need air. I head outside and jog through a slanting drizzle. Everything is difficult. Everything hurts. The contact of my feet against the earth sends sledgehammering blasts of pain through my joints. The fury, the rage, has been replaced with the urge, the lure, the powerful pull of steroids. I run into the heart of the beast of desire to kill it. My world is a potent cocktail of pain and desire. I push myself to run faster. I feel my chest explode in demand for oxygen. My feet slap against the concrete, my arms pump as hard as they can. *Run harder, motherfucker. Run.* The world zooms by.

Suddenly I'm tumbling forward and slamming into the concrete. I hear something crack. I don't know what it is. I don't care. My world is one white blast of obliterating pain and I am supremely happy. The urge is gone. I roll over onto my back on the slick concrete and stare up at the gray sky. The pelting rain obscures my vision. I feel like a wretched, feeble man who can't control his own desires. I think about the rain, the Buddha rain. I think about my sins. I think about the desire to be born again and about redemption. I think . . . I've been hearing a voice lately. I know it's not God. He died with my brother. But I'm overwhelmed by the presence. There's a beauty there. It's stronger than the urge. I think it's the voice of benevolence. I'm laughing . . . I'm crying. I'm lying in the gentle Buddha rain.

Week eight. I step on the scale fully dressed. I always weigh myself this way now. It's a stupid trick I play on myself so it won't seem

like I've lost as much weight. I'm like the anorexic who carries the huge, oversize purse so she'll appear small in comparison. I know it's a sleight of hand. But the numbers are important to me. Each lost pound has a psychologically debilitating effect. I'm that much less of a man.

I wonder, why am I wired this way? I wonder, can anyone help me?

It's week twelve. People are asking, "What happened to you, man? You look bigger on TV? Are you sick?" I want to smash their faces in. But instead, I put on a smile and respond, "I'm just leaning out, man," and act like it doesn't bother me. The truth is it's killing me inside. I've lost twenty pounds. I'm fucking shrinking! I'm drowning in a sense of powerlessness. A sense of defeat. It feels like I've been thrown into the ring with an opponent I know I can't beat. Each round I answer the bell, and each round the addiction beats the shit out of me.

I'm with a girl in a club and this guy is blatantly checking her out in front of me. I don't need 'roids to know what disrespect is. My eyes snap with anger. "Look, motherfucker," I say, "I'm gonna punch you in your fucking neck if you keep looking at my girl."

He smirks. He doesn't think I'm a threat. Twenty pounds heavier, this never would've happened. I know I can destroy him. I know I can slam his face into the concrete, knock his teeth down his throat, and make him eat his words. I *know* I can.

But that is no longer the measure of who I am as a man. I don't *have* that blinding rage. I don't *have* to do anything. I *can* walk away. It's not easy. Pride is a hard thing to swallow, but I walk away.

At week fourteen, I feel the grumblings of sexual desire, lust, returning to my body. It's just a flutter. But it's there. This is good.

It means my body is starting to produce testosterone again on its own after having been annihilated by the massive amount of steroids I've fed my system. I only hope I haven't destroyed it and my desire will be that of a normal man who hasn't obliterated and abused his endocrine system.

Week eighteen, I get together with a few of the other Gladiators. They're still huge and ripped. I'm jealous of their size and seeming invincibility. I feel inferior. I am the incredible shrinking man. I am not enough. I have to remind myself I'm heading to a place where I want to go. I am hosting, not competing. But the savage desire to compete and shine and be seen will not die. It goes beyond steroids. It's always been there. I don't understand why.

Why do I have to shine? Why do I have the need to be seen?

Each week, the culmination of events and happenings chips away at my resolve and the urge for 'roids grows. It's now more than a thirst. It's an insufferable hunger, a furious yearning that grabs me, punches me in the face, and won't let me go. This need for the drug overrides logic, the need for health, well-being, and sanity. I'm locked in the grand trap of steroids. I believe all my strength and courage, all my *glory*, is held in a pill and a bottle.

Still the need to find my authentic self is strong. Dan Clark is a fighter. It's been over twenty-two weeks and I'm still drug-free. I feel I can live this way . . . I feel I can live with everything I believe in being tossed up in the air for scrutiny. But as the start of season seven approaches—I realize what I can't live with. What I can't do. I cannot walk in front of an audience on national television without my security blanket, my silent killer, my best friend—steroids. Steroids are more than my crutch. They are my very feet. How can I walk onto national television, with a microphone in my hand, without my feet to carry me?

I start taking steroids again.

And again, it's for *just a little longer.*

The week before production is set to start, I bring all 230-plus pounds of my juiced-out self to visit my dad in the hospital. He is sick. He is a drug addict. Not the ugly kind who lives in darkness, in a cockroach-infested apartment, slamming a needle in his vein. He is the ugliest kind. The middle-class drug addict, addicted to prescription drugs. Vicodin. Fifty a day.

The second I walk in, I hate the place. It's too peaceful and serene. I think my father is pathetic. He is weak. He is an addict. I have no forgiveness in my heart for him. I don't want to be here. I come here out of duty. Not love. I enter his room and see him in the bed, tucked under the covers like a little baby. I don't know what to say to him. This is not his first time here. I feel the hate and apathy welling up in me. He thanks me for coming. I'm disgusted. I am uncomfortable. This is a man I feared and admired, a man I wanted to be just like. Now I despise him. He is weak and pathetic.

I am suddenly aware there is something . . . something tapping on the door of my subconscious. My dad is talking. I can't hear him. I'm searching for clarity, this nagging feeling, something I can't quite place. The tapping on the door becomes a sledgehammer smashing into my brain. It is lacerating. It is a familiarity that turns to shocking recognition.

I am just like him. I am an addict.

The nurse enters and starts talking to my father. I can't hear what she's saying. I see her lips moving, but the stunning revelation is overwhelming me.

I am an addict. I am just like him.

I have to leave the room to clear my head. "Hey, Dad, I forgot something in the car. I'll be right back," I say, and push through doors and storm out in the hallway. I walk. I stride rapidly along, deeply agitated. Feral. The words bang around in my head.

I'm an addict. I'm just like him.

I rifle through the similarity of our addictive drugs. Both prescribed by doctors. Both obtained illegally. Both abused. Both wreak havoc on our lives. My mind screams, *But I am not a drug addict!* He is. *My drug is different. My drug helps me do my job. His drug, his addiction, keeps him from functioning. An addict is someone who is weak and pitiful. An addict is* anyone *else in the world, but* ME.

I burst through hospital doors, spill onto the street and hop into my car. Tension creeps up the back of my neck until it throbs like a vise grip clamping down—squeezing. I'm raging inside. And I want the raging inside, I want the rushing to my brain, all of it—to stop. I pull onto the 405 freeway and drive. I have no idea where I'm going. I simply feel the need to move. Fast. There's a cluster of traffic. I blaze through it, music blaring as loud as it will go. The bass thumps and reverberates through my core. Still I hear the voice.

You're an addict. You're just like him.

I drive faster, more recklessly, trying to speed away from my diseased life. I finally take a breath and focus. I'm in front of the ancient downtown Los Angeles library. I'm not sure why I'm here. I didn't want to come here. I am just here. I am being led here . . . by something . . . by someone. But by what, I don't understand. I just know it's a presence bigger than I am. Something I can't speak of . . . but can feel. It is a benevolent force. Without judgment. I don't need to fully understand it. I only need to accept the guidance and listen.

I'm walking into the library. It's massive and old. I feel what I am: small and insignificant. I stride down the grand steps among the millions of books, floor upon floor of compressed knowledge. I glide through a door. My fingertips flick across binders as I move quickly and quietly through the great hall of books. Up one aisle and down the next, intuiting my way.

Abruptly I stop as my eyes snap toward a book. No. Something between the books. A pamphlet. I pull it out and level my breathing. *This is why I am here.* I set the small pamphlet down on a grand table, the dim light from above illuminating the cover: *Am I an Addict?* This odd little pamphlet isn't something you can check out. It doesn't belong in the library. It's been left here. Left here for me. One deep, steady breath, and I open the pamphlet. I silently rifle through it. The word *addict* blinks starkly at me.

> *Addict:* somebody who is physiologically or mentally dependent on a drug liable to have a damaging physiological or psychological effect.

A questionnaire begs to be filled out to see if one is an addict. I slowly answer the questions.

1. Do you ever use alone? [~~Yes~~] [No]
2. Have you ever substituted one drug for another, thinking that one particular drug was the problem? [~~Yes~~] [No]
3. Have you ever manipulated or lied to a doctor to obtain prescription drugs? [~~Yes~~] [No]
4. Have you ever stolen drugs or stolen to obtain drugs? [Yes] [~~No~~]
5. Do you regularly use a drug when you wake up or when you go to bed? [~~Yes~~] [No]
6. Have you ever taken one drug to overcome the effects of another? [~~Yes~~] [No]
7. Do you avoid people or places that do not approve of your using drugs? [~~Yes~~] [No]
8. Have you ever used a drug without knowing what it was or what it would do to you? [~~Yes~~] [No]
9. Has your job or school performance ever suffered from the effects of your drug use? [~~Yes~~] [No]
10. Have you ever been arrested as a result of using drugs? [~~Yes~~] [No]
11. Have you ever lied about what or how much you use? [~~Yes~~] [No]

12. Do you put the purchase of drugs ahead of your financial responsibilities? [Yes] [~~No~~]

13. Have you ever tried to stop or control your using? [~~Yes~~] [No]

14. Have you ever been in a jail, hospital, or drug rehabilitation center because of your using? [~~Yes~~] [No]

15. Does using interfere with your sleeping or eating? [~~Yes~~] [No]

16. Does the thought of running out of drugs terrify you? [~~Yes~~] [No]

17. Do you feel it is impossible for you to live without drugs? [~~Yes~~] [~~No~~]

18. Do you ever question your own sanity? [~~Yes~~] [No]

19. Is your drug use making life at home unhappy? [~~Yes~~] [No]

20. Have you ever thought you couldn't fit in or have a good time without drugs? [~~Yes~~] [No]

21. Have you ever felt defensive, guilty, or ashamed about your using? [~~Yes~~] [No]

22. Do you think a lot about drugs? [~~Yes~~] [No]

23. Have you had irrational or indefinable fears? [~~Yes~~] [No]

24. Has using affected your sexual relationships? [~~Yes~~] [No]

25. Have you ever taken drugs you didn't prefer? [~~Yes~~] [No]

26. Have you ever used drugs because of emotional pain or stress? [~~Yes~~] [No]

27. Have you ever overdosed on any drugs? [~~Yes~~] [No]

28. Do you continue to use despite negative consequences? [~~Yes~~] [No]

29. Do you think you might have a drug problem? [~~Yes~~] [No]

I scroll back over the questionnaire and tally up the score. Twenty-seven out of the twenty-nine questions I've answered yes.

"I'm an addict," I whisper to myself. I have a compulsive need and dependence on a drug. The pamphlet goes on to explain the seriousness of addiction and relates the lengths an addict will go to get and do drugs, regardless of the consequences. I think about the things I have blindly done:

Piss blood, fight, near heart attack, grow tits, fight, balls shrinking, fight, arrested, Mexico, fake Federales, fight, self-mutilation, GHB, fight, fighting to be a man.

The pamphlet says I have to say the word. I have to use the language of addiction. I have to put breath and voice behind my disease.

"I'm an addict," I say again.

I have to face the stark truth that I'm suffering through a relapse. I read that it is the only way to come to terms with my addiction. I am just like my father. The drug is different, but I am just like him. I am wretched. I am weak. I have a chemical dependency. I am an addict.

As big and strong as I am, I suddenly feel like a weak-willed and pathetic little man who can't control his own behavior. The shocking epiphany does not stop me from taking steroids, but it is the beginning of an understanding about my condition. I believe if I can allow myself to categorize what I am, then maybe it will be the beginning of a pathway to recovery.

Nitro escapes his death sentence and survives season seven. Going to the booth to do commentary is a natural progression; it happens in all sports. I'm comfortable with the microphone and happy to do it. And I'm thankful to Julie Resh and Rob Silverstein for keeping their word and making it happen. I am hosting. And I am *using*. I am a functioning addict, and that is something I have to live with.

American Gladiators' ratings may be on a slow decline in the United States, but it has become a smash hit around the world. Not only does our American version air in over forty countries, but England, Australia, Germany, Finland, and Japan do their own versions of *Gladiators*. It is especially HUGE in England, easily being one of the top-rated prime-time shows in the country. Nigel Lythgoe, the genius behind *American Idol,* is the producer.

Now London is calling. They want to do an international show in England with Gladiators from each of the countries competing against an international lineup of contenders. They want spandex. They want Nitro. I figure I have enough juice (literally) in the tank to don the suit one more time. Besides, I have always wanted to meet the queen and have a pint with her.

The English version of the *Gladiators* is everything the American version could've been and should've been. It's filmed in front of an audience ten thousand strong, who are whipped into a rabid frenzy normally reserved for soccer. What they do right, first and foremost, is make sure the Gladiators are huge stars. Nigel knows this is what drives the show, and he produces the shit out of it, just like he does with *American Idol*.

The Japanese version of the show is particularly important to me. I'm returning to my birthplace, the place I once denied being from out of embarrassment and the need to fit into my Caucasian world. I don't speak the language, but I want to learn it so I can go onstage in front of the audience and say, "I'm half-Japanese. I was born here. I am just like you." I'm always looking for a connection. A place to belong.

Japanese is an excruciatingly difficult language to learn. It takes months, but it's all worth it when I stand up in front of ten thousand people and speak in my native tongue. The house roars. They love being able to identify with me. They love knowing I am just like them. Well, almost. I'm a little different. I'm buffed out and blown up with a chemical assist. I've ingested enough steroids to stock a pharmacy and supply the East German swim team for a decade. My body is a minefield of needle marks from the years of abuse. I am just like them except I am Godzilla—a monster.

Back home, *American Gladiators* is on its last legs. It is dying. It never really recovered from the season-four loss of Gladiators during the negotiation crisis. Samuel Goldwyn is able to bleed an eighth season out of Johnny Ferraro's and Dan Carr's baby. Then it's done. *Gladiators* is over. But I'm still saddled with the big body. The addiction. I feel like a toy discarded by a kid who no longer finds it entertaining.

But that's okay, because Warner Bros. is calling. They want to do a movie with me. They tell me I'm the next big action star and put me under contract for three pictures. They bring in the producer from *Batman* to produce, and an Oscar-nominated editor to direct. This doesn't happen by accident. I've been striding toward this moment for years. I've hired and worked with the best acting coaches, and I've trained diligently for years with the legends in the martial arts world, all with the goal of becoming an action star.

Warner Bros. is heavily invested in the project, having spent over $500,000 on the Dan "Nitro" Clark movie. They tell me they're going to make it. They tell me I'm going to be the next Seagal, Van Damme. I know that no matter how much I prepare for life, it can never be scripted. But in serendipitous times like this, when it works just right, I think, *Life's a beautiful thing.*

Then the unthinkable happens.

The green-light guy at Warner Bros., the person who is God in the movie business and the person who can say yes and get a movie made, leaves. I am suddenly a stranger. The new green-light guy doesn't want anything to do with the old green-light guy's projects. He wants to carve out his own slate of movies. Call it collateral damage. My project is killed.

I'm crushed. More than crushed. I'm heartbroken. My lofty dreams are shattered. Suddenly the regimen of finding work in the business becomes grueling, frustrating, and futile. I don't have any emotional connection to it, my self-confidence has withered into a detached coldness. I feel like the world has no place for me. I am spinning into a crippling depression.

But then I find that life throws us opportunities in disguise. I'm suddenly filled with a savage desire to write. To tell stories. It's the only way to help fight the drugs. A couple of big problems.

One, I didn't finish college, barely went to class, and my writing skills are shit. Two, I don't know how to type. But I learn in six weeks. Six weeks of showing up at the computer and using the little appendages at the end of my hands to pluck away at the keyboard. I'm so used to using my entire body and physicality to accomplish everything, the daily ritual of finger-pecking is driving me insane.

But each morning I get up, flip the computer on, go to "Mavis Beacon Teaches Typing," and tap-tap-tap away. I buy a book about screenwriting by Syd Field. I read through it and think this might really be something for me. After all, I know the format from reading several scripts over the years in Hollywood. Writing is a learned skill like anything else. If I just stick with it, maybe I can one day actually make a living at it.

Armed with a new knowledge and desire, I start writing. The ideas, thoughts, and emotions pour out of me onto the page. I finish a screenplay about an aging wrestler, who just happens to be half-Asian, who has to team up with a group of kids to save the world. I think it's great. I get a few people to read it. Apparently it's not.

A second screenplay flows out of me about a cocky NBA basketball player who gets kicked out of the league. The only way back in is to coach a group of twelve-year-old kids at a community rec center. People actually like it. No one is buying. But I'm not done. I'm a fighter. I have a relentless desire to succeed. I keep writing. I do some small movie parts and a few commercials, barely enough to get by. I'm thirty-six years old and I'm a has-been. I'm contemplating getting out of the business and getting a regular-guy job. I've got so much pride and belief in myself, but I feel like I've been left behind and all the doors have closed. The best times in life suddenly seem so distant and unreachable.

I know the most dangerous time is when the world looks bleak. That's when the addicted voice fires up and coos in my ear, *Do you remember the good times? Do you remember how it feels to be a rock star?* And I believe that if I take the drugs again, the good times will follow.

A company calls and asks me to go to Lithuania to be in a movie playing a kick-ass Special Forces agent named Bear. I know they want Nitro. Not Dan Clark. I have a mortgage to pay, bills and child support. I agree, but I know the road to playing this part, once again, goes through my medicine cabinet.

It's been twenty years. Twenty years of steroid use. Twenty years of steroid abuse. Each time I do it, I'm disgusted with myself, but the lure is too much. It's like running into your high school sweetheart, who instantly brings you back to that time and place and those moments of lost youth. You feel the ache in the core of your being to be back in those times. You hook up with her, kiss her, fuck her, desperately grope for those lost moments until you realize they're gone and this is nothing but a pathetic attempt to taste the glory of youth.

And through the ups and downs, through the best of times, and the worst, there is only one constant. Steroids. And the mantra is always the same: Just a little bit to get me over the hump. Just a little bit for this job. Just *a little bit longer.*

I return to Los Angeles from Lithuania. I am home. I am alone. I lose it and begin to cry. Feeling like no one can help me out of where I am and I am helpless. I feel the shocking heat of my tears. I go to the bathroom and splash water on my face. I look up, and only a shadow of a man is staring back at me. I know I cannot quit steroids. I know I cannot get off the spinning wheel of this vicious cycle.

I'm having horrible nightmares. I don't know which way to turn. I am breaking down, both physically and emotionally. Lately, I find myself suddenly weeping in the strangest places. Tonight, while driving down Sunset Boulevard, for no reason, the emotion starts to swell inside me and the next thing I know, tears are spilling down my cheeks. I am sobbing so hard I have to pull the car over. And I have no fucking idea why.

I've seen men cry and I always think it is pathetic.

I cry. I'm pathetic.

I wonder how in the world I'm going to survive.

CHAPTER 22

The Toughest
Opponent of All

I sit across from her, all traces of my inner turmoil hidden away.

She looks at me with a piercingly interrogative gaze. "Why are you here?"

I'm unprepared. I've only come because I know I need to see someone. I've thought no further than that. "I'm not sure."

She's quiet. Gives me room to speak. But it's not words I feel lumped up in my throat. It's emotions. I fidget in my chair, uncomfortable. My eyes flick to the office wall. Anything to avoid her eyes, which are fixed on me. Plaques, certificates, diplomas, licenses, stare back at me. The collage of an entire life stuffed onto one tiny wall.

"So, how does it work? I just walk in here and tell you everything?"

"It works however you want it to."

I hate her answer. I want to wipe that snide look off her face. *You're the fucking therapist! I'm paying you! You tell me how it works! You take all those plaques and shit off your wall and shove them up your ass!*

I'm raging inside, but on the surface there is only a ripple. I smile thinly and take a leveling breath. I'm suddenly aware that I'm fidgeting and scratching my neck. I realize I'm afraid of this woman sitting across from me. She can't be more than five feet five inches and 120 pounds and she scares the shit out of me.

I can't beat her, I can't fuck her, I cannot charm her. I have to deal with her as she rips open the fabric of my soul, of who I am as a man. I know it's only going to be words and talking, but it feels so much like fighting. "Sad" is all I can say.

"You feel sad?"

"Yeah, all the time."

"Why?"

"I don't know . . . It's just always been there." I exhale deeply, let go a little.

Oh, shit, here it comes. There are not going to be any more words. I feel the emotion swelling, a torrent, a storm, an impossible surge. I draw in a stiff breath. Grit my teeth. Clamp my throat shut over it. *Please don't cry. Please don't fucking cry in front of her. I'm begging you. Don't cry!*

I fight back the emotion, fight to bury it back in that place. But then something cracks, some fissure opens behind the hard facade. A rogue bud of moisture escapes and spills down my cheek. But just as quickly, I wipe away the tear, ashamed. I can't look at her now. I am weak and pathetic. My knee is bouncing up and down like a jackhammer. I look down at my hand. It is trembling. I squeeze it into a fist. My entire arm starts to shake. It feels like a million volts are exploding through my body. *Control. Control it all.*

"It's okay. Let it go," she says.

Let it go. Is only seven letters long, but miles deep. *Let it go* is like telling a blind man to see, a crippled man to walk, a dead man to rise. *Let it go* is something I've never been able to do in front of a person since I was four years old, save for the drug-induced cry after my knee surgery twenty years ago. *Let it go* is something I cannot do.

It takes everything I have, but I slowly regain my composure and look at her. My eyes are steady, clear, resolute. I am a wall. This is a competition and I will not lose.

Startlingly, she leans forward and grasps one of my hands. For reasons I can't understand, every cell of my being electrifies. "Let me ask you something," she says, her eyes locking onto mine. "Why are you alive?"

I stutter and stammer, "I'm alive . . . I'm alive because . . . I don't know." Overwhelmed, trying to recover, I ask, "Why are you alive?"

"To *feel*," she says, her eyes, her entire being, filled with compassion. "It's what every atom of our body is built for. Without it, without love, without sorrow, life is just a ticking clock to death."

I try to speak but I cannot.

I am crying.

I am ugly. Weak. Pathetic. I've spent my whole life trying not to feel. Anytime an emotion seeps through the gates and rises to the surface, I grab it by the throat and choke the very life out of it. Now, I'm weeping openly in front of this woman I do not know. I am fragile and vulnerable. Everything in my body tells me to leave. To run. My heart tells me to stay.

By an act of will, I hold her eyes. To let her see me in my weakness—my ugliness, my humanness.

She tells me there is something beautiful in the fragility. Not to be ashamed.

She asks me to talk about what I'm feeling. When I try to speak, my voice squeaks. Words and tears will not come at the same time. She tells me to let the words ride on top of the emotion. It feels like another impossible task. I've already slit my soul open at its very core for her. Flushed with frustration, embarrassed, and filled with more emotion than I can bear, I tell her it's enough. I'm done for today. I don't understand that it's only tears. It's only being human.

"That's fine," she says, "we don't have to talk anymore. But I'd really like you to stay for a bit."

I know it's a trick. But I'm helpless against her. Deep inside, I know I need to be here. I know there's more.

Soon I'm talking. I'm telling her everything. I'm bleeding for her. I tell her things I've never told another human being. I tell her about my parents' divorce, crying on the plane as my mom disappeared through the door. I tell her about my brother dying in my arms. I tell her about watching my dad with two prostitutes when I was ten years old. I tell her about the fear I can't shake . . . about the voice . . . about the need to shine. I tell her I've spent a whole life trying not to feel. And I tell her about twenty years of steroid abuse. I tell her everything. I tell her about the fury and the rage and the fighting and the pissing blood and almost dying. I tell her about being limp-dicked and having tits ripped out of my chest and the pain and the aching joints . . . the destroyed knees and the injuries . . . and the pain . . . the addiction . . . my dad . . . the pain . . . the hate . . . the love . . . revulsion . . . my son . . . the desire . . . the craving to be a better man.

And I weep.

I tell her I beat my fist against the wall to feel. I tell her I hate what I've become, but I can't fight against it . . . I tell her about the rage . . . I tell her I am a monster . . . I tell her I want to do good . . . I tell her I've done all of this on my own . . . I am a monster . . . I am good . . . Beauty makes me weep . . . I tell her about the voice of benevolence . . . I tell her everything.

I look into her kind, compassionate eyes. They are brimming with tears. A profound beat exists between us. After a moment, she tells me to watch the movie *Ordinary People*. She believes there may be some commonality between the lead character, Conrad, and me. I tell her I've heard of the movie, but I'm not familiar with it. I ask her if it has anything to do with sports. She smiles and says it has nothing to do with sports or steroids. It's about *survivorship*. I'm not quite sure what she means. She says, we'll talk about it next time. Next time? Yes. I am coming back.

I drive to the video store. Something about the tears, about the purging, feels good. I feel empty and full at the same time. There's a warm contentment, but also an exhaustion. I feel like I've just fought fifty men. But as I pull into the parking lot of the store, I'm hit with a swift, sinking feeling in my stomach. I'm not sure what it's about. But something is wrong.

I enter Blockbuster and move down the aisle through the drama section. Now the dread has exploded into full-blown anguish. I pick up the video and look at the cover. Suddenly it hits me. I *know* this movie. It won the Oscar for Best Picture. Why didn't I remember it? It's about . . .

My mouth is suddenly dry. For a moment, I panic and forget to breathe. My hands are sweating. Yes, I remember this movie. It's been hiding in plain sight all of these years. *Ordinary People* is about a *teenage boy who blames himself for his older brother's death and tries to commit suicide to end his pain.* I think I am empty of tears, but without warning they start up again.

I sit at home alone in the darkness and watch the movie. Across my face flicker images of Timothy Hutton, who plays the younger, surviving brother. He's clearly broken—suffering from the guilt of having lived when his older, perfect brother died.

In the movie, a boating accident occurs in a stormy sea in the dead of the night. The brothers scream for each other to hang on to the capsized vessel until help arrives. The younger, weaker, not-so-perfect brother, Timothy, holds on. The older, perfect brother, whom Timothy tried to model himself after his whole life, does not.

He lets go. He dies.

Tears flood my eyes, blinding me as the stunning, eloquent

film finishes. I'm left with the words "People get hurt without anyone meaning it." I grip the pillow tightly and sob into it for a long time.

Timothy feels like he killed his brother. He feels like he let him down.

I know him.

He believes it has to be someone's fault. Or there is no goddamn point.

I know him.

He can't get over it. He can't get through it. It hangs over his head.

I know him.

He wishes he'd died with his brother. He doesn't want to face the world alone.

I know him.

He is me.

The mirror has been my friend and my enemy. I stand in front of it now in the naked morning light and it's neither. It's simply there. I am simply here. I take a good long look at my reflection and try to figure out who I am. I am searching for an identity that goes beyond my physicality. I know I'm no longer an athlete, a Gladiator, or a juicer. I wonder who the hell I am. I study my battle-scarred face and the scars across my nipples. I ask myself, has the journey been worth it? Where do I go from here?

For our second session, I slide into the office chair, feeling comfortable, already an expert after one visit. I'm healed. I'm not even sure why I've come here again. It's amazing how quickly I can distance myself from the truth.

We talk about the movie. I tell her it was moving and profound, and though our struggles are similar, it is "only" a movie and the younger-brother character and I aren't that similar. I am sad. I feel guilty. But I'm not a loner and I haven't tried to kill myself.

She looks me square in the eye. "What do you call taking steroids for twenty years?"

I'm thunderstruck. I don't know what to say. I open my mouth to form words, but nothing comes out.

"How many opponents have you faced over the years on *Gladiators*?"

Without hesitation I answer, "Probably over five hundred."

"The most awful truth about self-denial is that one doesn't even know they're buried in it, because the deceptions of self are so absolute."

I nod at her. Wonder where she's going with this.

"I think you've faced over five hundred opponents, but you haven't faced yourself."

I'm awed by the profundity of the statement.

Faced over five hundred opponents, but never faced myself.

She tells me facing myself will be the toughest battle, and until I do that, I will always have a problem with chemical dependency.

"How do I do that? How do I face myself?"

"How do you think you do that?"

This is such bullshit. I'm not in the mood for riddles. "I understand what you're saying, but I don't really get it. Self-acceptance is facing myself. What do you mean?"

"What do you think I mean?"

"You know what? This isn't fun! Just give me the answers?" I say angrily.

She sits back, patiently clasps her hands together, and gently puts them on her lap.

This smug little bitch. I feel violence flooding in.

"What are you feeling right now?"

I lie. "Nothing. I'm cool."

"You don't feel anything?"

"Nope."

"Addressing your feelings is important for you. You've learned to lock away all your fear, anger, and hurt. It's not healthy."

"Okay, you really wanna know?" I lean forward. "I'm pissed. I wanna smash your fucking face in."

She recoils involuntarily. Blinks, clears her throat. "Why are you angry?"

"Because you've got the fucking answers, and you sit there on your smug little ass and make me suffer. It's like I'm fucking drowning and you've got the lifeline and you won't throw it to me!"

I've frightened her. She tries to hide it. Instantly I feel bad. Like a monster who needs to scare and intimidate.

"Look, I'm sorry. It's just that I'm kind of screwed up and I need some help making sense of some things going on inside of me. Things I'm feeling." I pause and try to collect my thoughts. "It's like . . . I feel like . . ." *Searching. Searching. How do I find words for what's going on inside me?* "It feels like . . . I'm standing on a wind-beaten precipice at the end of the world, and if I don't find something to hold on to, I'm going to fall off."

She leans forward. "I think you need to look at the original incident that caused your guilt. It's similar to what happened to Ray Charles and Johnny Cash. Ray Charles watched his little brother die. Johnny Cash was goofing around when his older brother died. Both blamed themselves for their brothers' deaths. Both were wracked by survivor's guilt. Both turned to drugs and alcohol as a way to deal with their pain. Both teetered on the verge of destruction until they faced this."

I sit back in my chair and let my hands drop in my lap.

"You can call it the curse of the surviving brother. The surviving brother agonizes over why he was chosen to live. He has to constantly prove his worth, because he's living for two."

A chill shoots up my spine. Time suddenly stops. The seconds, the minutes, the hours, as I stare into the face of a truth I didn't know existed.

THE SURVIVING BROTHER AGONIZES OVER WHY HE

WAS CHOSEN TO LIVE. HE HAS TO CONSTANTLY PROVE HIS WORTH, BECAUSE HE'S LIVING FOR TWO.

I'm shattered into a billion tiny fragments, swimming in an endless moment of cathartic revelation. It's like someone has flung open the curtains, streaming light into a dark room. There is a loss of control. Everything is lost in the light. I collapse into the truth. Losing myself. Finding myself. Vulnerable, emotionally naked, exposed like I have never been before.

Bathed in the bright light of acute clarity, I begin to see clearly. I suddenly understand my father. He never got a chance to go through the catharsis of healing. The world drops away. It's just me. I'm an island of understanding. I understand my father. I understand the cancer that ate away at him. The wound that never healed. I forgive him.

Guilt is the cancer my father couldn't beat until it killed him. He died from an accidental overdose of methadone, taken within prescription limits. It was sudden, it was tragic. He was fifty-seven years old. He was hooked on Vicodin and was taking the methadone to help get him off the Vics. My dad was a beautiful man. He just didn't see it himself. He medicated to stop the pain. The pain of losing a child. The fragility of the human spirit amazes me, but so does the catharsis of grief. I know what killed him. It wasn't the drugs. It was the guilt. He never learned that tears and misery are necessary for the catharsis of grief.

I go home that night and I dream.

I'm back in Vietnam with my brother on the rooftop in the black of night. I relive the accident. There is a shower of sparks. My eyes glisten with terror. Randy is slammed back against the wall. I reach over and try to help him up. I rush to the wall. I scream. There is no one. Please! Someone help me! HELP ME! I scream and scream until my lungs bleed and I am coughing and hacking.

The world suddenly gives over to blackness. Then it's just my brother and me on the rooftop. He's lying on the ground, burnt badly, bleeding, dying. I'm crying. Sobbing. Begging him not to die. Then suddenly I reach out and touch his face and I know he's dead. He is a corpse . . . cold and inert. His lips are blue, his limbs completely limp, and his fingers are burnt back to stubs. I slump down onto the ground and sob. A hand reaches and touches my shoulder. The touch is comforting. I look up and see myself as a grown man.

I whisper faintly, "It's not your fault. You did all you could."

The young me seems set free by the revelation and begins to weep. I reach out and pull him into my chest. He collapses into me. I hold him. I hold me. We stand there for a long moment, two human beings, bonded together against the world.

In 1993, my father went back to Vietnam and recovered
my brother's remains. I didn't go. I didn't need to. Since my brother
died that fateful day, he's always been with me. I feel him now.

CHAPTER 23

The Road Back

"Here. Try some of these," he says to me, holding out a handful of pills.

The act seems eerily similar to what started the madness years ago. "What are they?"

"An herb and vitamin complex. They'll help your body recover naturally from all the years of steroid abuse."

I don't believe him. No vitamin is strong enough to reverse the damage. No herb is potent enough to bring back what was lost. Nothing can help me.

"Just try it! You'll like it!" he says with the zeal of a preacher.

I stare at him long and hard. Over the years I've met hundreds of guys, hundreds of pill pushers, who always have some kind of natural miracle pill or cure. But nothing that can help bring back what steroids have stolen from me. This is something I have to live with. Each and every time I took a steroid, it was my decision. My fault. No one is to blame but me.

But I'm not complaining. In some ways I'm glad I took them.

I'm glad they fucked me up. I'm glad I made the mistake. So maybe others won't have to.

Bleary-eyed, I take the palmful of pills from the guy and swallow them in one gulp.

"Great!" he says with a little too much enthusiasm. "You should feel better right away. And after thirty days, you'll be amazed at the difference! It'll change your life!" He shakes my hand and hands over a month's supply of the pills. "Remember, you said you'll write me a testimonial for my website!"

I smile and nod my head that I will, if they work. He doesn't know this is a futile exercise. I will never write him a testimonial because the shit does not work. I'm tired of none of this shit working. I want a shot right now. My body aches. I don't care if I feel like shit afterward. I don't care if I feel guilty. I don't care! I don't care! I don't care! *Feed me.*

I'm raging inside, but I go home like a docile, henpecked bitch and go through the mundane exercise of taking the concoction. I do it faithfully every day like a preacher praying at the pulpit. And every day I hope there will be an inkling of the promised change. And each day, I don't feel shit. But still I do it, like I have on the thousands of other days since I've been clean.

How important is it?

It's everything.

This is the road to recovery. This is the fight back to health. It's trying a thousand different pills and remedies in hopes that something will rejuvenate my steroid-annihilated endocrine system. It's eating green shit that I can't pronounce the name of. It's repeatedly getting a tube shoved up my ass by a woman like Olga, to try to cleanse out any lingering toxins. It's keeping up on all the latest enzymes, vitamins, and exotic concoctions from all over the world. It's getting hundreds of needles jabbed in me by an acupuncturist to open the meridians. It's being on the edge of science. It's being willing to try anything because I know my joints are destroyed beyond repair—I know I'm stuck with scars on my face, the telltale map of my rage—but I believe there is hope for my body and my general sense of well-being. I believe there is still a chance for me to be healthy.

This struggle, this beautiful agony, reminds me I'm alive.

It's different, but it's the same as it's always been. I'm taking a pill to counteract a pill or drug I've taken. It's my Sisyphean fate. I'm the guy who is condemned to repeat forever the same meaningless task of pushing a giant boulder up a mountain, only to see it roll downhill again. How I feel the effects of the natural remedies is what has changed. With steroids, the results scream like a runaway train and hit you smack you in the mouth. That is why they are so addictive. That is why they are so toxic. The results of these new concoctions are barely a whisper.

But I do it every day.

Every damn day.

Because I know the alternative. I've been down the treacherous steroid path. I always thought I could handle it. But the drug handled me. Easily and completely. At my peak, I was six feet two, 260 pounds. Muscles stretched and defined by red, white, and blue spandex. I loomed as if I blocked out the sun. That was everyone else's perception of me. But I was never big enough or strong enough for myself. I reached a point where contentment and fulfillment were impossible. Steroids could never fill what I was missing inside.

I've learned steroids are a hopeless reach for happiness.

I *used* as an express route to fame and glory, and to enhance the physical body. The trouble is that there came a time when steroids stopped giving me things and started taking them away. My body rose up in protest: *You are destroying me.* But with the coming of each new day, raw, bleak, and chill, I knew I couldn't stop. Steroids are my addiction, my alcohol, my cocaine. They have always been there for me. They gave me courage, they gave me aggression, they helped me reach new highs. But they also *destroyed my body.*

How do I explain the obsession to anyone who hasn't experienced it? If there is a steroid in the house, I know it won't last longer than a stolen brownie at a Weight Watchers clinic. It isn't an instant, overwhelming punch in the face of desire like what I hear heroin or meth is. It's a slow pull, a tug that turns into an all-out flood of desire.

It took twenty years for me to find the fortitude to quit. It took my body breaking down. It took the realization that I was an addict and that the scar tissue from when I was a kid never got a chance to heal. It took the words of my therapist.

Good man. Bad problem.

I was suffocating. These words were my oxygen. They allowed me to separate myself from the drug and know that the voice of benevolence I hear and feel in my heart is real. It allowed me to see that I have a problem, not that I am the problem. It allowed me to believe in the possibility of God.

FOR NOW, I'VE BEATEN IT. I'M CLEAN. BUT BY NO MEANS DO I THINK IT'S OVER. The stark reality is, saying that you're done and actually being done are two different things. I know I'll always struggle with the desire to take steroids, just like an alcoholic struggles with his desire to take a drink. And the land mines of temptation are everywhere.

In the summer of 2007, Country Music Television (CMT) calls and asks to me to participate in a celebrity bull-riding show with bull-riding legend Ty Murray. The first thought isn't *Oh, shit! They want me to ride a two-thousand-pound bull! I could die!*

It's *Maybe I should get some Deca and do a quick cycle so I look good for the camera.* This is the obsession. This is the addiction. I want to give the audience what they expect. I want to be huge and ripped. I want heads to turn. I want people to gawk. I want. I want. I want.

Then I have to have the *conversation.*

I have to talk myself off the ledge. It is a simple dialogue. I only have to take a literal step to remember the cost. That is when the pain shoots up through my knees. I only have to rise from sitting—

that's when the pain tears through my lower back and hip. I only have to pull off my shirt and look in the mirror—that's when I see the scars across my chest. I only have to lean in close and gaze at the reflection of my face—that's when the seven scars of rage stare back at me. I only have to be intimate with a woman—that's when, many times, I need a pill.

It's a sobering exercise. But I have to do it. I have to have the conversation *all* the time. It's the only way I can stay clean.

I see a doctor friend of mine who casually asks me if I want a shot of testosterone. Casual and harmless like "Do you want cream and sugar with your coffee?" So harmless, I break out in a cold sweat and my heart starts palpitating in anticipation. I lick my lips, I can taste the glory.

Then I have the conversation.

It happens a lot at the gym, when there's a guy next to me, throwing up an insane amount of weight on the bench or the squat rack. He's huge and ripped; his muscles glisten with sweat. I feel the envy . . . I feel the urge to be that guy swelling up in me. But it's also tinged with empathy. I feel sorry for the guy. I know the pound of flesh it's going to eventually cost him.

The biggest test happens in the fall of 2007 when NBC calls me to consult on the new *American Gladiators*. I know I'm probably the foremost expert on the show. I know I can contribute to the production. I know I can be of value. I just don't know if I'm enough. I feel the flood of desire. I feel the ache.

I hang up the phone and look at my hand. It's shaking from excitement and fear. I'm excited about the prospect of sharing my knowledge to help the revival successfully usher in a brand-new audience. Fearful of the prospect of returning to my old way of life. It's so much more than a phone call. It means facing the past. It means facing age. It means facing a world that once ruled and defined me, and I don't know if I can do it without by best buddy—steroids.

On a grim Saturday morning, I go so far as to call a buddy

from the gym and ask him to look around for some Deca for me. He hesitates before responding. He knows I've been clean for a long time. "Are you sure?"

I say that I am. Then I lie, a transparent lie: "It's not for me. It's for a friend."

I meet him a week later in a grimy alley behind a liquor store to do the deal. As I sit in my parked car among the graffiti and trash, I feel like what I am. Weak and pathetic. I feel a wave of nausea pushing at the back of my throat. I swallow quickly a couple of times. I can't believe I'm back here again after all these years. Fortunately, he is five minutes late. Just enough time for me to come to my senses. I figure it's a sign telling me to leave. To not do it.

I start my car. At that exact moment, he pulls up next to me and gets out of his car. I keep thinking I'm going to tell him the deal is off. I've changed my mind. It's over. It's more than over. I'm pissed. I'm pissed he's letting me do this to myself. I'm pissed this bastard, who is supposed to be my friend, is willing to sell me drugs.

He strolls over to the window and holds out the bag. I stare at him, then calmly hand him the money and go home. There is no protest, no denial, no rage. Simply obsession. I return home and load a syringe full of Deca, flick the tube to knock the air bubbles out of it, and hold it up in the gleaming light. I'm having the conversation, but no one is listening. *Hey! Remember how bad this shit is for you! Remember it destroyed your body! Take a step! Look at your reflection!*

I swab my glute with an alcohol pad and slam the syringe into my ass. I try to depress the plunger to unload the oil deep into my muscle, but my fingers won't let me do it. The conversation is screaming in my head. *Don't! Stop!* But I keep trying, and for the life of me I can't do it. I can't depress the plunger. My body has risen up in revolt and will not let me take the shot. The next thing you know, I'm leaning over the toilet, throwing up. That's how violent the reaction is. That's how deep the wounds are.

So much of the road back is finding a place where I belong. It's about finding an identity, figuring out my place in the world, and how I can contribute. There has got to be more for me than "I used to be a Gladiator."

In the best-case scenario, maybe I can be *hope*. Hope that by going through the trial by fire, I can teach others. Hope that my ugliness can become my beauty and I can go from a destroyer to a creator. Hope that by speaking frankly about steroids, by opening the vein and going deeper, I'll be able to sway a teen kid from taking them. Hope that somehow and in some way I can help.

The thing is, it feels really good to say I'm clean. One of the gifts of being clean is that the humanity . . . the life rushes back in. With this humanity comes the desire to communicate. To tell my story as a way of detoxifying it. I felt a similar yearning a few years ago in another blush of clarity when I started to write, to scratch at the surface of my soul. I didn't even know how to type. In high school, I stubbornly refused to take typing. I was so sure I'd never need such a pedestrian skill. I didn't know that the simple act of tapping my fingers on a keyboard would be my lifeline.

But now I see that the story of my time as Nitro on *American Gladiators* is a candid, eye-opening account of the dangers—both known and unknown—of steroids as viewed through the lens of my twenty-year affair with the drugs. What began when I was a freshman in college to speed up recovery from an injury turned into an all-consuming addiction that has left me scarred both physically and emotionally, yet ultimately on a path of personal discovery and redemption.

But it's more. It's a story about identity, about finding my place in the world and trying to make sense of my older brother, my protector, dying in my arms when I was ten and he was twelve. It's about trying to fill a gaping hole inside me. It's about never really feeling safe after the death of my brother. It's about the fragility of the human spirit and my belief that if I built up my body and became an impenetrable mound of muscle, nothing would ever hurt me. The bigger I got, the less chance anything had of penetrating my tough exterior; the less chance I'd have to actually feel anything. My body became my armor, my fort, my defense against the world—in order to survive, to protect that little boy inside who was told so many years ago that big boys don't cry.

I was untouchable. I was a prisoner.

Now I'm free to live as a father, a student, a teacher, a writer, and a fully conscious human being who can feel. Finally, I no longer have to punch walls and bloody my knuckles just to prove to myself that I'm alive. And I no longer have to lie.

These days, when I hear someone say, "Big boys don't cry," I hear a voice inside me answer, "I know. But men do."

Epilogue

When I look back on these years, it all seems like a beautiful nightmare. Some kind of gothic, spandex-laced, Tim Burton, otherworldly adventure—singed in a blustery red, white, and blue. Memories creep through me at the most unexpected times. The magnificent cheers of the crowd, the eternal voice of Mike Adamle rumbling over the loudspeakers, the glare of the lights as we sprinted onto the arena floor, crashed into contenders, and thrust our fists in the air in victory.

I remember how it ended, in a shroud of darkness on an empty soundstage. All of our lives have spun in different directions since then, but we were part of something. We were a team swathed in the colors of our great country, and we wore them with honor and dignity. We were warriors who would do *whatever* it took to win.

But times have changed. Steroid use, once a dirty little secret confined to locker rooms, sports-medicine clinics, and gyms, has now erupted into a national controversy that has tarnished the reputations of some of the nation's most revered sports heroes. The very suggestion that an athlete might have cheated his or her way to a championship or a spot in record books ignites passionate debate and uncovers raw emotions and a sense of national betrayal.

I say let the past go. Focusing on the past will not solve the problems of the future. To help a country in crisis we need to devote every ounce of our energy toward prevention—toward saving future generations from falling into the insidious web of addiction.

How can we help future generations? After more than twenty years of abuse, I've witnessed it all, not only with the cunning eye of a user, but also with the clear eyes of someone drug-free, and here are my conclusions:

- We need to even the playing field with strict, rigorous testing in all collegiate and professional sports. I'm also a proponent of testing high school students for drugs. It's the only way to really make inroads.

- We need to punish offenders with swift and severe suspensions, sending the message loudly, clearly, and decisively: "Cheaters will be punished." Because as long as steroid users are being awarded scholarships and huge contracts, people will be inclined to cheat. The real tragedy is those whose dreams were crushed because they didn't take steroids.

- We need to educate the next generation of possible steroid users/abusers about the harmful side effects and addictive potential of steroids. One of the best ways to do this is for past steroid abusers to stand up and tell their stories. Maybe through the solace of shared experience we can help steer a few teenagers away from these harmful substances.

The difficult part is, no one wants to hear the truth about steroids before he or she takes them. I didn't. Despite all the negative information that's available, young athletes are still embracing steroids with a passion. It's easy to understand why. All teenagers are thinking about is improved performance and unlimited success—gold medals, home runs, touchdowns, a place in history.

They don't want to know about breast tissue growing beneath their pectoral muscles, infertility, liver failure, brain cancer, or sexual dysfunction. They don't want to hear about the anger either—the uncontrollable and sudden bouts of 'roid rage.

We also need to wade through the *ocean of lies* told by some current steroid abusers to justify their usage. One of the biggest lies steroid users tell is *there is no such thing as 'roid rage.* I've heard a lot of chatter saying, "If you're a jerk before steroids, you'll be an even bigger jerk on steroids. But if you weren't, then you won't have a problem when you're on them." This is simply not true. The physical altercations and bouts of rage I describe in this book are just a peek inside Pandora's box. My face carries the rest of the tales of my rage. I have a scar that slices down from under my nose to the top of my upper lip that prompts some people to ask if I had a cleft lip as a child. I have another beauty under my bottom lip, too, and one that splays across the underside of my chin; not to mention two scars under my left eye and a nose that's been broken enough times that people assume I'm a professional boxer.

I wasn't the only one who got into fights. I've witnessed countless other incidents when guys were on the juice. I've seen fifty-pound dumbbells thrown across the gym and heads rammed through wooden doors. I watched a juicer friend of mine rip a guy out of a car through the window simply because the guy cut him off on the road. I've seen a fellow Gladiator, who at five feet ten tipped the scales with 285 pounds of ripped muscle, pick a guy up off the ground by the neck and slam him just because the guy stepped on his shoe. I also remember an incident in college when two of our biggest and strongest lineman, both weighing close to three hundred pounds, showed up at practice with their faces bruised and bludgeoned after getting into a fight with each other, even though they were best friends.

Fighting and smashing heads through windows is just the tip of the iceberg when it comes to 'roid rage. It goes miles deeper. An unusual number of bodybuilders (the ultimate steroid abusers) are behind bars for homicide.

Bertil Fox, a former Mr. World, is incarcerated for the murders of his girlfriend and his girlfriend's mother.

Southern California bodybuilder John Riccardi awaits execution for a double homicide.

Another California muscleman, Gordon Kimbrough, is serving twenty-seven years to life for the murder of his fiancée.

Former police officer and hard-core bodybuilder James Batsel is serving a life sentence for murder, shooting his victim nine times.

A female strength prodigy, Sally McNeil, is also serving life for the murder of her bodybuilder husband.

Bodybuilders are not the only offenders. Anyone who uses steroids is prone to homicidal rage. When professional wrestler Chris Benoit tragically strangled his wife and suffocated his seven-year-old son, then hung himself on June 25, 2007, his long-term use of steroids came to light.

Psychiatrist Harrison Pope of McLean Hospital in Massachusetts sometimes serves as an expert witness in court. He claims to have been involved in a dozen murder cases where someone using steroids—despite no previous history of violence or a criminal record—killed somebody. In one case, a sixteen-year-old boy was charged with killing his fourteen-year-old girlfriend. Pope says, "We have no evidence of any criminal or violent activity before he started taking steroids. At that point, he had a series of run-ins with the police, which culminated in the murder."

Another steroid lie: *once you get off the juice, the aggression disappears.* Not so, according to a recent study at Northeastern University. Long after more than one hundred hamsters were taken off steroids, the aggressive tendencies continued in 85 percent of them. Autopsies revealed steroids actually damaged the hamsters' brains. Even after steroids were discontinued, their anterior hypothalamus, known to regulate aggression, continued to pump out more of a neurotransmitter called vasopressin, which induces aggression.

Maybe this is why I still feel the fire of competition boiling in my blood and why a part of me will always miss hitting someone, will always miss the violence. I used to believe I was just wired this way. Now I suspect I've damaged the wiring in my brain with steroids.

One of the most insidious lies is *steroids help athletes recover from injuries more quickly.* The opposite is actually true. Injuries increase when on steroids. Look at baseball in the steroid era between 1992 and 2001. According to baseball doctor Bill Wilder in *ESPN the Magazine,* "The number of players on the DL rose from 352 to 465, a 32% increase. Days spent on the DL went from 17,920 to 27,779." Players were also hurt more severely. Days spent on the DL per injury increased 55 percent over that span. And injuries that were rarely problems before all the bulking up were now common: patellar tendonitis, strained rib cages, torn hamstrings—the kind of stuff that happens when oversize muscles rip away from bones that can no longer support them. The kind of stuff that happened to me when I tore my hamstring.

The biggest steroids lie of all? *Steroids don't kill.*

Maybe we should ask Lyle Alzado. Or professional wrestlers Eddie Guerrero, Curt "Mr. Perfect" Henning, Ravishing Rick Rude, British Bulldog Davey Boy Smith. Ask bodybuilders Mohammed Benaziza and Andreas Münzer, who both competed in the Arnold Classic. Ask, seventeen-year-old Taylor Hooton, a baseball player from Plano, Texas, or twenty-four-year-old baseball player Rob Garibaldi, who both committed suicide due to depression brought on by steroids. Or maybe we should ask my good friend and SAE fraternity brother from San Jose State Ken Caminiti, the three-time All-Star and 1996 National League MVP. Or better yet, let's ask famous steroid guru Dan Duchaine, who wrote the extremely popular *Underground Steroid Handbook,* a book that became the bible for those wanting to use steroids, who died an untimely death in 2000 at age forty-eight from complications of kidney disease. The question that begs to be answered, if he was so smart and knew how to take steroids safely, why is he dead?

These deaths captured the public's attention because the victims were high-profile people. I know that we'll never hear about countless other deaths attributed to steroid use. Yet, even in the face of these tragic deaths, pro-steroid pundits still deny the connection. They'll say Alzado died of a brain tumor, there's no correlation. Caminiti was on painkillers. This bodybuilder died of dehydration, that wrestler died from something else. But the sobering truth is the one thread that ties all the deaths together is *steroids*.

Over the years I've also learned steroids are a *gateway* to other psychotropic drugs. After you've crossed the line and taken an illegal drug, it's a lot easier to say yes to a line of blow, a tab of ecstasy, or a puff off a joint. You've already taken drugs to alter the way you feel. What's one more? On second thought, steroids are more than a gateway; they are an expressway to abuse. On steroids your motor is going so fast, and you've got so much energy and aggression gunning through your system, you've got to find a way to release it. I'll go even further and say I don't know a juicer who hasn't tried or doesn't use other illegal drugs.

More than anything else, parents need to know how to deal with the subject of steroids with their children. I agree wholeheartedly with the leading recommendation of most rational antidrug campaigns. Talk to your kids often and early about steroids. If not, you're leaving their education in the hands of someone else. One of the biggest problems is that a kid sees Barry Bonds. He's forty-four. To a sixteen-year-old, that's more than a lifetime from now. I once heard a kid say, "I'm seventeen years old; forty-four is an old man. I don't care if I'm dead then." This shortsighted thinking makes it difficult for parents and puts the challenge square on the shoulders of the powers-that-be to stop drug use at the highest levels. We can't ask our children to avoid steroids if the athletes they admire use them with impunity.

No matter what anyone says, like it or not, professional athletes are role models and are setting the bar for younger kids. The trickle-down effect is immeasurable. As U.S. surgeon general Richard Carmona told the press, the problem of steroid use is "less a moral and ethical issue than it is a public health issue. If youngsters are seeing their role models practicing this kind of behavior and it seems acceptable, then we need to do something about that because it is a health risk." This is why it's crucial we stop steroid use in pro sports. Nothing less than our children's health is at stake.

And parents shouldn't think their children are safe because they aren't into sports. Recent studies show that teenagers use steroids to change their physical appearance, and alarmingly, the segment of the population with the fastest growth in taking steroids is teenage girls. The Centers for Disease Control estimates that around 7 percent of high school girls have tried steroids.

Dr. Charles Yesalis, a retired Penn State professor and a recognized authority on steroids, estimates that "at least half a million and probably closer to three-quarters of a million children in this country have used these drugs in their lifetime." Adds Yesalis, "The teens I've talked to say [steroids and HGH] are as easy to get as marijuana." The Mayo Clinic has published information that one-tenth of U.S. steroid users are teenagers.

Another major concern about kids and steroids is the manner in which the youngsters procure the drugs. Because sales of steroids and growth hormone have been pushed underground, kids are buying them off the Internet or from some gym junkie. The drugs they're getting are the rejected veterinary crap and the imported garbage from Mexico. If these kids were using the best stuff, that would be bad enough, but it's worse because they're using the terrible, toxic stuff.

How do you know if your kid is on steroids?

Look for rapid weight gain and increased musculature. If the child suddenly adds ten to twenty pounds of hard-forged muscle, know something is wrong. Also look for an outbreak of acne, especially on the back and chest. Pronounced mood swings, irrational rage, irritability, and an obsession with muscle magazines could be another clue to steroid use.

To protect your children from the dangers of steroids, you need to be vigilant. You need to read the labels of vials and containers you find in your kid's room, drawers, and cabinets; and investigate the contents. A child should not be able to get away with telling parents that steroids are vitamins. You need to be on the lookout for *nandrolone decanoate, stanozolol, Dianabol, Winstrol, tamoxifen, clenbuterol, clomifene,* and *oxandrolone,* for example. There's also a wealth of easily accessible good information for parents on the Internet. The best prescription is to know your child and trust your instincts. They are rarely wrong.

When confronting a child about steroid use, you need to treat it the same way you would any other illegal drug. It's just as serious, addictive, and dangerous. Your stance needs to be strong, definitive, and prohibitive. You also need to understand the specific intricacies of steroids and know that coming off the juice can be fraught with medical and psychological complications. A doctor should be consulted. In extreme cases, such as Taylor Hooton's, the problems can lead to depression and suicide.

With all of the overwhelming information on the toxicity of anabolic steroids, I'm amazed and sickened that some people out there, such as Jose Canseco, still advocate the use of steroids. I'm appalled and frightened when I consider the effects that his popular book *Juiced* have had on the American psyche, particularly that of the younger generation.

The eyes of the world are focused on this. It's up to us to pull together as a nation and conquer the steroid crisis that is crippling sports and our society. We now know the extent of the problem. Everyone is culpable. No one can look the other way. Through the telling of my story, I hope that my experience will discourage others from taking the dangerous and destructive steroid route. Just as Nitro pioneered a unique and powerful kind of physical fitness and confidence, I hope that with this book Dan Clark will lead others away from becoming victimized by a cycle that will destroy their health and happiness. We've all felt the effects of the cycle. Now it's up to us to save today's youth from sacrificing an entire life so as to become a hero for less than fifteen minutes of fame.

I didn't write this book as a diatribe or an exposé, but to tell my story. It's a simple one. I was injured on the football field, took steroids to recover, and got caught in a web of addiction that took me twenty years to overcome. Don't let this be your story or the story of your child.

Acknowledgments

With the last name of Rumble, how could my editor, Brant Rumble, be anything but the perfect editor for my book? Immeasurable thanks to you, Brant, for your invaluable guidance, and trusting me to write the book on my own. I would also like to thank the entire team at Scribner—Brian, Heidi, Anna, Ashley, Amber, Rex—for making the experience so pleasurable.

An immense wave of gratitude goes out to my manager, Joel Gotler; agents David Vigliano, Michael Harriot, and Kirby Kim; with an assist from attorney Peter Dekom.

Special thanks to Andrea Cagan for her invaluable wisdom and wise words, as well as Kathy Tomlinson for her sharp eye and helpful insight.

A big thank you to Michael Easton. You're a prince.

Thank you Bo Zenga, Tag Mendillo, Brad Boyer, Karen Lutz, and Gary Goldstein.

Thank you Starbucks store 11991 for the hospitality and the warm cup of joe.

To Kathy Savitt and Michael Lennon, Greg and Sharon Maffei, and my other friends on Orcas Island, thank you for making Orcas a home away from home.

And with my boundless love, thank you Gay Jodi Rosenthal. You are my rock and inspiration.

To my family and friends, you're everything to me. You are like the air I breathe.

Last, thanks to my son. I love you more than you'll ever know.